THE HURRICANE
PREPAREDNESS
HANDBOOK

THE HURRICANE PREPAREDNESS HANDBOOK

Bob Stearns

Skyhorse Publishing

Skyhorse Publishing books may be purchased in bulk at special discounts
for sales promotion, corporate gifts, fund-raising, or educational purposes.
Special editions can also be created to specifications. For details, contact
the Special Sales Department, Skyhorse Publishing, 307 West 36th Street,
11th Floor, New York, NY 10018 or info@skyhorsepublishing.com.

Skyhorse® and Skyhorse Publishing® are registered trademarks of Skyhorse
Publishing, Inc.®, a Delaware corporation.

Visit our website at www.skyhorsepublishing.com.

10 9 8 7 6 5 4 3 2 1

Library of Congress Cataloging-in-Publication Data is available on file.

Cover design by Jane Sheppard
Cover satellite image of Hurricane Rita by NASA
Cover photographs, bottom: FEMA News Photo

Print ISBN: 978-1-63220-275-8
Ebook ISBN: 978-1-63220-941-2

Printed in China

Contents

Foreword

I experienced my first hurricane at age nine on August 1, 1944, in Wilmington, North Carolina. It was a nameless Category 1 with 90-mile-per-hour winds, not really very much of a storm by the yardstick of severe hurricanes that have occurred over the last two decades, but it nevertheless served at once both to frighten and fascinate me. A continuing interest in weather eventually led to my obtaining a degree in meteorology in 1958, and then serving as a navy weather officer for the six years that followed. I spent my last three years on active duty forecasting hurricanes for the navy. This included working, and occasionally flying with, the Navy Hurricane Hunters, an aircraft weather reconnaissance squadron stationed in Puerto Rico for the purpose of monitoring tropical storm activity in the Atlantic basin. Military hurricane reconnaissance has since been reassigned to the Air Force.

After leaving the navy in 1964 I spent the next four years as a research associate on a hurricane research project with the University of Miami's Rosenstiel School of Marine and Atmospheric Sciences. I spent a lot of time flying into a great many hurricanes with the National Oceanic and Atmospheric Administration (NOAA) Research Flight Facility as part of that project.

However, flying inside a hurricane in an airplane designed for that purpose and going through the same storm on the ground are vastly different experiences. Once the aircraft has completed its mission it can then leave the storm with its turbulent ride many miles behind and quickly retreat to a quiet location. But when the storm comes to you and you're confined to a house, you have no choice but to hang on and hope that you will survive the long ordeal that lies ahead. I continue to find this prospect far more terrifying than bouncing around in an airplane for a few hours!

The purpose book is therefore twofold: (1) To provide some insight and understanding about how these monster storms work, and (2) to provide you with the knowledge that will help you make the necessary preparations to ensure the safety and survival of yourself and your family, as well as to reduce damage to your property as much as possible.

—Bob Stearns
Jupiter, Florida

CHAPTER 1
The Nature of the Beast

If you live within 100 miles of the Atlantic or Gulf of Mexico coast, you are very much at risk when a major hurricane comes ashore in your area. The closer to the coast, the greater the risk. But if you understand what hurricanes are, how the warning system works, and how to prepare for them, your odds of survival increase enormously. The same goes for your ability to protect your property.

Ever since modern man evolved on this planet, severe hurricanes have proved over and over again to be the single most catastrophic event nature has thus far sent our way. They are worse than tornadoes (which can be stronger but are far smaller and much more short-lived); even worse than tidal waves (tsunamis), earthquakes, or volcanic eruptions—at least those we have experienced since the beginning of recorded history. It doesn't matter whether you call them hurricanes, typhoons, or tropical cyclones, over the course of history these huge, extremely violent windstorms have caused more human deaths and more widespread damage than almost all other natural disasters combined.

Some terrifying examples: As recently as November 13, 1970, an extremely severe tropical cyclone slammed into the lowlands of East Pakistan (now known as Bangladesh), killing at least 500,000 people. Some unverified estimates raise the number to almost one million. A storm on October 7, 1737, did the same in Bengal, India, causing more than 300,000 human deaths. And yet another 300,000 or more unfortunates were also killed in Hiapong, Vietnam, in 1881.

Damage in Mississippi by Hurricane Katrina in 2005. *FEMA photo by Marty Bahamonde.*

Why did so many die in these storms? Lack of sufficient warning is undoubtedly the single most significant factor. In situations like these, geography can also be a major contributing feature: low-lying shorelines with an extremely high human population density (still true today around the Bay of Bengal) are exceedingly vulnerable to storm surges, which have been recorded even in modern times to exceed 20 feet and reach many, many miles inland. During and after a major hurricane, water (flooding and storm surge) kills far more people and causes far more damage than the strongest winds. Hurricane Katrina (2005) in New Orleans is a prime example of the terrible delayed flood damage that can follow a major hurricane.

Even in recent times there have been storms with fatalities totaling in the many thousands. Hurricane Mitch hit Honduras in October 1998, a Category 5 with 165 mph winds, officially leaving at least 9,086 dead in its wake. But the true total from that catastrophe, by some estimates more than 20,000, will likely never be known because of the remoteness of the region and lack of an accurate census.

In 2005, Hurricane Wilma, a Category 5 storm with maximum winds of 185 mph and a minimum central pressure of 882 millibars (a new record for Atlantic hurricanes), slammed into Mexico's Yucatan Peninsula, almost a direct hit on the resort city of Cancun, before moving on to cross South Florida as a Category 3 with

125 mph winds several days later. The total damage in the United States was more than $20 billion, yet only 22 U.S. deaths were attributed to Wilma. Everyone knew it was coming almost a week before it arrived and had plenty of time to prepare.

I visited Cancun four months after Wilma, and even in that short time the area had made a surprising recovery. I observed a number of wrecked vessels of all sizes on nearby reefs—the most visible evidence of the storm—and some damaged buildings were still under repair. Thanks to advance warnings from both the U.S. and Mexican governments, fatalities were significantly reduced in that country and structural damage was not nearly as severe as it otherwise could have been.

Compare Hurricane Wilma's fatalities to the worst hurricane ever to hit the United States in modern times, at least considering the human casualty total: the Great Galveston Hurricane, which smashed into that low-lying Texas coastal city on September 9, 1900, as a Category 4 with maximum winds of 145 mph. It killed an estimated 12,000, mostly by drowning. Lack of warning was the reason so many died; no one even realized such a massive hurricane was out there until it suddenly came ashore at daybreak.

Since that dreadful day, the number of human casualties in the United States, and to a significant extent in all the other developed nations around the Atlantic basin,

HURRICAN
ANDREW

NWS MIAMI RADA
August 24, 1992
08:35 UTC 04:35 ED

dBZ
> 48
48　　Hurricane
45　　Research
42　　Division
40
37
34
31
29
26
23
20　　NOAA/AON
18　　Miami, FI
15
< 15

Domain: 100 x 100 kn

Fig. 6. Low-level radar reflectivity pattern (dBZ) obtained at 0835 UTC fro last full sweep of the National Weather Service's Miami WSR-57 rada (located at the "+" identifying the National Hurricane Center [NHC] before Hurricane Andrew demolished part of equipment. Open whit circle near coast indicates site of peak storm tide shown in Fig. 7

Hurricane Andrew making landfall just south of Miami on August 24, 1992. *NOAA photo.*

has declined dramatically as the hurricane warning system has steadily improved. Another factor in human casualty reduction, and steady decrease in hurricane damage (relative to what would have happened other-wise) is a better understanding of what these storms are, and how to prepare for them. Improvement in building codes in most U.S. coastal counties, especially since the debacle of Hurricane Andrew in 1992, is also a contributing factor.

Hurricane Andrew came ashore just south of Miami, Florida, during the predawn hours of August 24, 1992, with maximum sustained winds of 170 mph and gusts to at least 200. It was the first Category 5 storm to hit the United States since Camille struck Louisiana with 190 mph winds in 1969, and at that time Andrew was also the most destructive hurricane ever to strike the United States. It did a total of $31 billion damage to Florida and Louisiana, yet the core of its most destructive winds was only 20 miles wide, and it moved rapidly along an east-west track across the Florida peninsula right over the city of Homestead (20 miles south of Miami), which meant it came and went in just a few hours. Had Andrew come ashore directly into downtown Miami, both the damage and the human casualty figures would almost certainly have been higher.

One of the principle reasons for the high damage in southern Dade County was lenient building codes at that time. Miami had been lucky for 27 years; the last major hurricane to hit South Florida was Betsy in 1965, a Category 3 storm with maximum winds of 125 mph that came ashore on Key Largo 40 miles south of Miami. And only one year earlier, Hurricane Cleo actually scored a direct hit on downtown Miami as a Category 2 with 105 mph winds. But damage from neither

Betsy nor Cleo was extreme in the Miami area, further contributing to a general sense of complacency.

And because of this extended lull in hurricane activity along the southeast Florida coast, local homebuilders had constantly lobbied for less rigid construction codes to save on rapidly rising costs. But the reality is that cheaper homes are weaker homes. And unfortunately, some of the construction was also downright shoddy, as evidenced by Andrew's total destruction of many homes built during the 1980s.

When Hurricane Andrew arrived, I was living in a house a few miles south of Miami, right on the northern edge of the storm's path of major destruction, but also far enough inland not to be at risk from storm surge. My house had been built in 1968, a concrete block structure with substantially reinforced wooden gables and shingle roof. At the time of its construction the Dade County building code was still strong, and in spite of winds gusting to 150 mph or higher in my neighborhood, my house suffered no damage. I had prepared for Andrew by covering all the windows with heavy sheets of plywood, which did exactly what they were supposed to do—keep the storm outside. Incidentally, most of the older homes in Andrew's path that had been properly prepared came through with little or no damage, while a great many of those built between 1980 and 1992 literally blew apart.

Still, there were only 26 deaths attributed to Andrew in Florida and 54 in the entire United States, despite the fact that after bashing Florida it crossed

Damage south of Miami by Hurricane Andrew (Category 5, 1992). *FEMA photo by Bob Epstein.*

the eastern Gulf of Mexico and went ashore two days later in central Louisiana as a Category 4 with 135 mph winds.

The total damage caused by Andrew could have been even worse had it not been for a warning system that predicted its Florida landfall several days in advance. Still, the bottom line is that many residents, new to the area and having never faced a major hurricane, failed to take these warnings seriously. Some even attended so-called hurricane parties instead of getting ready. If everyone had done what they should have, damage would have been substantially less and likely even fewer lives would have been lost.

After Andrew, another 12 years passed before the Florida peninsula suffered any significant hurricane damage. Then came 2004, the start of a very active two-year period that began with Charley, a Category 4 storm with 145 mph winds that plowed into the south-west coast and moved straight up Charlotte Harbor, on August 14. Next came Frances, a Category 2 with 110 mph winds that struck the middle of the East Coast in early September, followed a few days later by Ivan coming ashore in the northern Gulf of Mexico as a Category 3 with 120 mph winds. Ivan continued northeastward into Virginia, then emerged from the East Coast where it looped southward to eventually come ashore in south Florida as a very annoying and still very wet tropical depression with 30 mph winds.

But Florida's latest rash of hurricane troubles did not end with Hurricane Ivan. Hurricane Jeanne came ashore in the middle the peninsula's East Coast on September 26 as a Category 2 storm packing 120 mph winds. Total damage from all these 2004 storms was in excess of $31 billion.

In 2005 major hurricanes Cindy, Dennis, Katrina, and Rita also battered the northern coast of the Gulf of Mexico repeatedly. Katrina was in its early stage of development when it hit South Florida with 90 mph winds before emerging into the Gulf of Mexico and headed north to destroy a major part of New Orleans and a large section of coastal Mississippi. Hurricane Wilma closed out that season when it came ashore in southwest Florida on October 24 as a Category 3. The total U.S. damage was in excess of $93 billion along the northern Gulf Coast alone, plus another $20 billion for Wilma in Florida, bringing the final total to more than $113 billion. The official death toll in the United States from Katrina was 1,833 (mostly in Louisiana and Mississippi), making it one of the deadliest in years. The 2005 Atlantic basin hurricane season was the most active in more than 100 years, with a total of 15 hurricanes and 13 tropical storms between June 8 and the end of the year.

Yet, in spite of long-range advance predictions of above-normal activity for both the 2006 and the 2007 hurricane seasons, they actually turned out to be below average with no major storms coming ashore anywhere in the United States. The bottom line? As of yet, making long-range predictions of hurricane activity before the beginning of a coming season is still very much a work in progress, so don't take anything for granted until the season is officially over. After all, the 2005 hurricane season turned out to be far worse than the pre-season long-range predictions.

The Bottom Line

Hopefully some real lessons have been learned (or perhaps re-learned) from the recent hurricane disasters of 2004, 2005, and 2012. Two storms in particular stand out for different reasons. First is Hurricane Katrina in 2005, a Category 3 storm with winds of 125 mph, and a death toll of over 1,800, and enormous flood damage in the Lower Ninth Ward of New Orleans—damage that to this day is still is not completely repaired. Second is Superstorm Sandy, a huge but barely Category 1 hurricane that morphed into a monster post-tropical storm as the eye made landfall near Brigantine, New Jersey on October 29–30, 2012.

Even though Sandy barely had winds over 70 mph as it came ashore, its huge size allowed those winds to blow unimpeded across hundreds of miles of open ocean to create huge seas and a storm surge of 7 or more feet in some areas. To make matters even worse, this surge coincided with high tides of 6 to 7 feet along the shoreline north of the eye, flooding hundreds of miles coastline from Atlantic City, New Jersey to Massachusetts. The eastern end of Long Island suffered a storm surge of 3 to 6 feet and 4 to 9 feet (all above ground) in Staten Island and Manhattan. Sandy's enormous destruction totaled nearly $50 billion and took 72 lives.

Bottom line: *preparation is everything!* Being properly prepared offers your best chance of survival, as well as the best way to protect your property—which in turn enhances your odds of survival. The two are interconnected.

And that is just what the rest of this book is all about.

CHAPTER 2
How Hurricanes Form

Hurricanes are not at all like the familiar northern-latitudes winter storms (strong low-pressure systems) that bring cold fronts southward during the winter months. Those non-tropical tempests get their energy from an infusion of cold air, and are therefore known as cold-core systems.

Instead, hurricanes get their energy from warm, moist tropical air, which makes them warm-cored. This warm, moist air primarily comes from the ocean surface when it has been heated by the sun to temperatures of 78 degrees Fahrenheit or higher. The higher the sea surface temperature, the more energy is available for the development and intensification of the storm.

The mechanism works like this: An area of disturbed weather causes warm, moist air from the ocean surface to rise rapidly. As this heated air rises, it cools and its water vapor condenses to form rain clouds. This process of condensation releases heat energy called the later. heat of condensation, which warms the cooler air aloft.

and thus causes it to rise. This rising air is replaced by even more warm, humid air from just above the ocean below. And so the cycle continues, drawing more warm, moist air into a developing storm, which continues to get more and more heat from the sea surface below. The end result is a low-pressure system with a wind that circulates around it in a counterclockwise direction.

In the beginning the low is weak, with a minimum pressure not much different than the surrounding atmosphere. But soon the rain, and sometimes thunderstorm activity, begin to increase in intensity, and the area covered by this bad weather begins to enlarge.

In the northern hemisphere, the circular winds around low-pressure systems move in a counterclockwise direction, slowly spiraling inward toward the center. Because the central pressure of a developing tropical system at this early stage is only slightly lower than its surroundings, the winds are light. But as the low deepens (the central pressure decreases), the winds get progressively stronger. And as the wind field around the low strengthens, so does the rain activity around the center.

Once the wind flow around the low-pressure system has formed a complete circle, it is called a tropical depression and is assigned a number in the sequence for that year. If the low continues to deepen, the winds become progressively stronger; once they reach a maximum of 39 mph, the system is officially designated a tropical storm and gets the next available name on the alphabetical list for that hurricane season.

If the low still continues to deepen, when the maximum winds reach 74 mph it officially becomes a hurricane (for example, Tropical Storm Greta is renamed as Hurricane Greta).

Many years ago hurricanes were referred to in the official records by their date of landfall. By the middle of the twentieth century, they were designated by sequential numbers for that year; then from 1950 through 1952 by letters of the phonetic alphabet (i.e., Hurricane Able, Hurricane Baker, and so on). Finally, in 1953, women's names were substituted, and in 1979 the World Meteorological Organization and the U.S. National Weather Service switched to a list of names that also included men's names. The current list of names recycles every six years, unless the name of a particularly severe hurricane is retired. We will never see another Andrew, Katrina, or Wilma, even though those names may have been used several times in prior years for tropical storms or hurricanes that did not became "famous."

As the storm or hurricane continues to grow, the rain activity intensifies to cover an expanding area. Strong thunderstorms can form within this band of heavy rain, but not all hurricanes are accompanied by significant thunderstorm activity. And some have less rain than others. A hurricane with less total rainfall than usual is called a "dry storm" by meteorologists, b there is always some significant rain activity within every tropical storm or hurricane.

Often, the wettest hurricanes are not the strongest in terms of wind. But if they are accompanied by extensive rain, and if they move slowly enough, the flooding potential escalates, as the slow forward motion provides longer exposure to the rain shield as it passes over a

Infrared satellite image of Hurricane Katrina in the Gulf of Mexico, August 2005. Katrina was a Category 5 storm with 175 mph winds at this time, but fortunately had decreased to a Category 3 with 125 mph winds by the time it made landfall. *NOAA photo.*

given location. The end result can be massive flooding in those areas most susceptible to water accumulation. Hurricane Irene, which came ashore on the southern tip of Florida in 1999 with 75 mph winds, was a prime example of a wet storm, although it was barely strong enough to be classified as a Category 1 and wind damage was slight. But it dumped up to 20 inches of rain in the Miami area in 24 hours, which caused extensive local flood damage—even though it was not accompanied by any significant storm surge.

The Making of a Hurricane

Even the most severe hurricane has modest beginnings, essentially as an area of disturbed, rainy weather somewhere over one of the tropical or subtropical oceans of the world. For the purposes of this book we will be talking about hurricanes that originate over the Atlantic Ocean north of the equator, as well as the Caribbean Sea and the Gulf of Mexico. This total area is generally known as the Atlantic basin.

An area of disturbed weather can develop from a non-tropical low-pressure system that drifts over warm, tropical water, or by the remnants of a cold front that does the same. Or it can begin as one of the many large rainstorms that generate over equatorial Africa and drift westward into the open Atlantic Ocean near the Cape Verde Islands as tropical waves. Eventually one of these disturbed areas will mature into a tropical depression with a low-pressure center and a weak counterclockwise wind circulation, and a hurricane is born.

Historically those disturbances that originate near the Cape Verde Islands have the greatest chance to grow into major hurricanes, primarily because they cross thousands of miles of warm, open Atlantic Ocean before making landfall. The trip can take a week or more, offering plenty of time for intensification. This typically takes place from late August through early October when atmospheric conditions are just right, and these monsters are often referred to as Cape Verde hurricanes.

As long as it remains over sufficiently warm water, and unless shearing upper level winds do not cause it to weaken, the hurricane always has a chance to grow. If the conditions are right, a weak hurricane can develop explosively into a real monster in 24 to 48 hours. Hurricane Katrina did this over exceptionally warm Gulf of Mexico waters in August of 2005, blossoming from an 85 mph Category 1 into a 165 mph Category 5 monster in 48 hours. Fortunately for those impacted along the north Gulf Coast, it had weakened to a 125 mph Category 3 by the time it came ashore, or the damage (bad enough as it was), could have been a lot worse.

Hurricanes vary not only in intensity, but also in size. The most intense are not always the biggest. Even though Hurricane Andrew, when it hit South Florida in August of 1995, was a Category 5 with almost 200 mph winds, it was a relatively small storm. Its satellite signature (visible associated cloud pattern) was perhaps only 200 miles in diameter, and the radius of hurricane force winds (74 mph or greater) was around 100 miles in diameter. By comparison, Hurricane Floyd, a Category 5 with 155 mph winds that trashed the Bahamas in 1999 (and fortunately was only a minimal Category 1 by the time it made landfall in North Carolina), had a satellite signature more than 700 miles in diameter at its peak.

Strong hurricanes may go through one or more strengthening/weakening/strengthening cycles, as did Katrina in 2005. It was a Category 5 for only 18 hours. Hurricane Wilma, also in 2005, was a Category 5 for just 24 hours, but a Category 4 with maximum winds of 135 to 150 mph for two days. After that it cycled between a Category 3 and 2 several times before it hit southwest Florida. At this stage in the development of hurricane forecasting, it is much easier to predict the movement of a storm for three or more days than it is even to guess what the intensity of that storm will be 12 hours later.

There are some weather scientists who suggest that because of the current trend in global warming the tropical sea surface temperatures are increasing as well. Some of these same scientists predict that because of sea surface warming we will see more hurricanes in years to come, and a greater percentage of these will become Category 3 or stronger.

However, not all meteorologists agree. Recently, another group has published findings that would seem to indicate just the opposite. They feel global warming is actually inhibiting hurricane formation by increasing unfavorable, shearing upper-air wind patterns. Let's hope this theory is right.

We do know from years of experience that an El Niño (a disruption of the ocean-atmosphere system in the Tropical Pacific that increases sea surface temperatures along the equator with important consequences for weather and climate around the globe) inhibits hurricane formation in the Atlantic basin by creating upper level winds that cause strong shearing of the storm's internal structure. Statistically, El Niño years produce fewer hurricanes in the Atlantic, but at the same time they cause more hurricanes in the eastern Pacific off Mexico through increased sea surface temperatures.

On the other hand, those same statistics also reveal that during La Niña years (cooler than normal equatorial surface water in the Pacific), there are more hurricanes in the Atlantic and fewer in the eastern Pacific. The El Niño/La Niña patterns reverse themselves roughly every six or seven years, with some neutral years in between. These patterns are not precise, and the ability to forecast these changes, while improving, is still a work in progress.

Once a tropical depression, tropical storm, or hurricane has formed, its forward motion depends upon the atmospheric currents in which it is embedded, much like a chip of wood floating along on the surface of a river. I'll explain more about forecasting in Chapter 4.

Where Hurricanes Form

Depending upon the time of year, there are defined areas where most hurricanes and tropical storms tend to form, and these areas shift around the Atlantic basin on a month-to-month basis throughout the June-through-November hurricane season.

During June the primary area of origin is the southern Gulf of Mexico and the northwestern Caribbean. From there these storms typically move toward the north, ranging from northwestward to northeastward, making landfall somewhere along the Gulf of Mexico shoreline from Mexico to Florida. Fortunately this month does not usually see the development of many storms.

By July the area of origin has expanded considerably as the sea surface begins to warm, and storms can form just about anywhere in the Gulf of Mexico, the western Caribbean, the Bahamas, or the western tropical Atlantic. Most commonly they make landfall around the western Caribbean, the Gulf of Mexico, or occasionally somewhere along the U.S. Atlantic coastline. Some also stay well offshore of the Atlantic coast and follow a curving track that takes them in the general direction of Bermuda. Usually there is a somewhat higher probably of storm formation in July than during June.

Historically, August begins the most active part of the hurricane season. Storms during this month form mostly throughout the western half of the tropical and subtropical Atlantic and occasionally the central Gulf of Mexico, threatening the entire Caribbean, the Gulf of Mexico, the U.S. East Coast, and the North Atlantic in general.

The hurricane season peaks sharply around the middle of September. This is the month during which the most storms and strongest storms form. This is also the month during which the greatest number of the real monsters of the hurricane world start somewhere just west of Africa and become the dreaded Cape Verde hurricanes. As mentioned earlier, they have lots of time to strengthen as they move westward over a tropical ocean that is at its yearly warmest. All of the Caribbean, Gulf of Mexico, and the entire U.S. East Coast is vulnerable to any storm that forms this month.

By middle to late October the number of storms is usually on the decrease, although the 2005 season (the most active on record with a total of 28 named tropical storms and hurricanes) made a strong departure from the norm by producing three hurricanes (including Wilma, a monster Category 5 with the lowest barometric pressure ever recorded in an Atlantic hurricane and maximum winds of 170 mph), and four tropical storms—the last of which was named Tropical Storm Alpha because there were no more human names

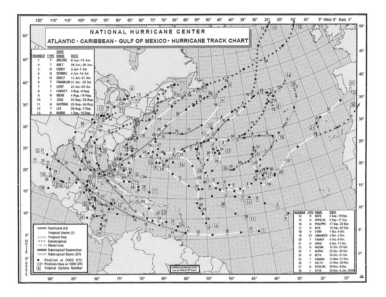

Hurricane and tropical storm tracks for the 2005 season, the busiest on record. *Courtesy National Hurricane Center.*

available for that season. Most October storms form in the western Atlantic, the northwestern Caribbean, and the southern Gulf of Mexico. For this reason the area around Mexico's Yucatan Peninsula is frequently called Hurricane Alley.

Typically the end of November brings an end to the active Atlantic hurricane season, and in some years none form during the entire month. But now and then a strong storm or hurricane manages to develop in the Caribbean or the Bahamas to threaten the Yucatan, peninsular Florida, the Bahamas, or the islands that make up the northern perimeter of the Caribbean.

It is not uncommon for a tropical storm or even a hurricane to form during December, but these mostly develop in the central and far eastern Atlantic where they wander around aimlessly and inconvenience shipping without ever making landfall.

The Atlantic Hurricane Season

The Atlantic Basin Hurricane "season," which actually includes the North Atlantic Ocean, the Caribbean Sea, and the Gulf of Mexico, officially starts on June 1 and ends on November 30. During that time there are daily summaries and discussions of the weather in the

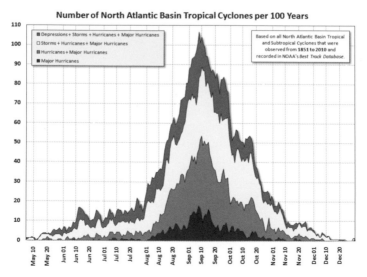

Number of North Atlantic Basin Tropical Cyclones per 100 Years

tropics issued by the National Weather Service. Areas of disturbed weather are specifically noted and carefully monitored for potential cyclone development.

As you can see from the graph below, the season starts with very little activity on June 1, and eventually peaks around September 11 or 12. From there it declines steadily until November 30. The period of most intense activity typically occurs from mid-August to the last week of October. But just because the "official" season ends before December does not mean hurricanes cannot occur during the "off" season. In fact they have occurred during every month of the year, but fortunately they rarely occur from December through May.

CHAPTER 3
Hurricane Intensity

The Saffir-Simpson Hurricane Wind Scale is a 1 to 5 rating system that describes hurricane intensity, and it is intended to provide an estimate of the potential for property damage and flooding that can be expected from that particular hurricane's landfall. Wind speed is the determining factor in this scale, as storm surge values are highly dependent on the slope of the continental shelf and the shape of the coastline in the landfall region. Note that all wind speeds use the U.S. one-minute average. The scale was developed in 1971 by civil engineer Herbert Saffir and meteorologist Bob Simpson, who at the time was director of the U.S. National Hurricane Center (NHC).

Category 1

Wind: Winds 74 to 95 mph (64 to 82 knots or 119 to 153 km/hr).

Water: You can expect a storm surge that is generally four to five feet above normal.

Damage: Usually there is no real damage to building structures, but expect at least some damage primarily to unanchored mobile homes, shrubbery, trees, and possibly even to poorly constructed signs. Also, there can be some coastal road flooding and minor pier damage.

Reference Storms: Hurricane Lili of 2002 made landfall on the Louisiana coast as a Category 1 hurricane. Hurricane Gaston of 2004 was also a Category 1 hurricane that made landfall along the central South Carolina coast. The damage profiles from both fit this category.

Waves on top of a storm surge increases the damage potential considerably. *Bob Royall photo.*

Category 2

Wind: Winds 96 to 110 mph (83 to 95 knots or 154 to 177 km/hr).

Water: The storm surge is generally six to eight feet above normal.

Damage: There will be some roofing material, door, and window damage to buildings. Expect considerable damage to shrubbery and trees, with some trees blown down. Also expect extensive damage to mobile homes, poorly constructed signs, and piers. Coastal and low-lying escape routes can flood two to four hours before arrival of the hurricane center. Small craft in unprotected anchorages can break free of moorings.

Reference Storms: Hurricane Frances of 2004 made landfall over the southern end of Hutchinson Island, Florida, as a Category 2 hurricane. Hurricane Isabel of 2003 made landfall near Drum Inlet on the Outer Banks of North Carolina as a Category 2 hurricane. Damage caused by both fit this category.

Category 3

Wind: Winds 111 to 130 mph (96 to 113 knots or 178 to 209 km/hr).

Water: The storm surge is generally 9 to 12 feet above normal.

Damage: There will be structural damage to small residences and utility buildings, with some potential for building wall failures. Expect considerable damage to shrubbery and trees, with foliage blown off trees, and also some large trees blown down. Mobile homes and poorly constructed signs will be destroyed. Low-lying escape routes are cut off by rising water three to five hours before arrival of the center of the hurricane. Flooding near the coast destroys smaller structures, while battering from floating debris can damage larger structures. Terrain continuously lower than five feet above mean sea level may be flooded inland as much as eight miles (13 kilometers) or more. Evacuation of low-lying residences within several blocks of the shoreline may be required.

Reference Storms: Hurricanes Jeanne and Ivan of 2004 were Category 3 hurricanes when they made landfall in Florida and in Alabama, respectively, with damage that fit this category.

Category 4

Wind: Winds 131 to 155 mph (114 to 135 knots or 210 to 249 km/hr).

Water: Storm surge will generally be 13 to 18 feet above normal.

Damage: There will be much more extensive building wall failures, with some complete roof structure failures on small residences. Shrubs, trees, and all signs are blown down. Expect complete destruction of mobile homes, as well as extensive damage to doors and windows of other buildings. Low-lying escape routes may be cut off by rising water three to five hours before arrival of the center of the hurricane. The storm surge will do major damage to lower floors of structures near the shore. Terrain lower than 10 feet above sea level may be flooded, requiring massive evacuation of residential areas as far inland as 6 miles (10 kilometers).

Reference Storms: Hurricane Charley of 2004 was a Category 4 hurricane when it made landfall in Charlotte County, Florida with winds of 150 mph. Hurricane Dennis in 2005 struck the island of Cuba as a Category 4 hurricane. Damage caused by both fit this category.

Category 5

Wind: Winds greater than 155 mph (135 knots or 249 km/hr)

Water: A storm surge generally greater than 18 feet above normal can be expected.

Damage: There will be complete roof failure on many residences and industrial buildings. Some buildings will be completely destroyed, and small utility buildings blown over or away. Almost all shrubs, trees, and signs will be blown down. Expect complete destruction of mobile homes, as well as severe and extensive window and door damage to other buildings as well. Low-lying escape routes are cut off by rising water three to five hours before arrival of the center of the hurricane.

There will be major damage to the lower floors of all structures located less than 15 feet above sea level and within 500 yards of the shoreline. Massive evacuation of residential areas on low ground within 5 to 10 miles (8 to 16 kilometers) of the shoreline may be required.

Reference Storms: Only three Category 5 hurricanes have made landfall in the United States since records began: The Labor Day Hurricane of 1935, Hurricane Camille in 1969, and Hurricane Andrew in August, 1992. The 1935 Labor Day

Hurricane struck the Florida Keys with a minimum pressure of 892 millibars—the lowest central pressure ever observed in a hurricane in the United States. Hurricane Camille struck the Mississippi Gulf Coast, causing a 25-foot storm surge, which inundated Pass Christian. Hurricane Katrina, a Category 5 storm while over the Gulf of Mexico, was responsible for at least $81 billion of property damage when it struck the U.S. Gulf Coast as "only" a Category 3. It is by far the costliest hurricane ever to strike the United States. In addition, Hurricane Wilma in 2005 was a Category 5 hurricane at peak intensity while in the central Caribbean and is the strongest Atlantic tropical cyclone on record with a minimum central pressure of 882 millibars, although it had decreased to a Category 3 by the time it reached the United States.

Category 6

As yet there is no Category 6, although some weather scientists have recently expressed concern that the current trend toward global warming may someday create monster hurricanes of such great strength that an additional category for winds over 200 mph may be needed. I, for one, fervently hope I am no longer around if this ever comes to pass!

Keep in mind that all of previously mentioned property damage described for each category is caused by wind alone. But in the end by far the most damage and also the greatest number of human fatalities are caused by water: flooding and storm surge. This is precisely why warnings to evacuate low-lying and coastal areas should always be taken very, very seriously.

And always remember that a hurricane or tropical storm can dramatically increase in intensity in just a matter of hours. Which means that if the warning indicates it will make landfall as, for example, a Category 1, it certainly could be much, much stronger when it finally gets there just a few hours later.

CHAPTER 4
Forecasting Track and Intensity

During the 1950s when I was a student working toward my degree in meteorology at Florida State University, hurricane forecasting was almost entirely a matter of hands-on experience. The better forecasters were those who had been at it the longest and had the best understanding of what these storms were all about. There were no computer models to work with, no mathematical equations to predict movement. In fact there were no computers available as forecasting tools in the sense we understand them today. The computers of the day were nearly the size of a small automobile, only capable of sorting pre-punched data cards at a high rate of speed. Even the least expensive desktop computer available today is light-years ahead of those early models when it comes to any form of data processing and number crunching.

There were also no weather satellites back then, so we had to depend entirely upon surface observations and weather balloon data for upper atmospheric conditions collected by forecasting offices and military weather stations scattered around the United States, plus a few throughout the Caribbean and Central America, and some ships at sea—and a small but fearless group of Navy and Air Force aviators we eventually came to know as the Hurricane Hunters. These observation aircraft, augmented in the 1960s by NOAA research aircraft that also carried scientific equipment and highly trained crews, were our only eyes in the sky when it came to locating storms far out upon the trackless expanse of a very big ocean.

Back then, even using aircraft to locate the center (eye) of a storm many miles from shore was not easy.

NOAA hurricane research aircraft in flight. *NOAA photo.*

There was no Global Positioning System in those days, and the range of both Loran and airborne radar was limited. Once out of range of all of the then-available electronic navigation aids, we had to rely on dead reckoning and the skill of the onboard navigator, who also utilized celestial navigation when the sky was visible (which it often wasn't for many hours at a time). The fact that we spent many hours of each long flight banging around in heavy weather certainly did not help. All of this also made wind speed estimates difficult, since those were mostly determined by observation of the sea surface from an altitude of 500 feet or less. So if our position estimates were within 20 miles of the storm's actual location, that was considered pretty good.

But location errors also made forecasting even more difficult. Often, 24-hour hurricane landfall predictions were off by 50 to 100 miles. So were their arrival times, sometimes by many hours. If you don't know exactly where a storm is located is start with, how can you accurately predict precisely where it will go and when it will get there?

The advent of high-powered computers and the development of mathematical models of storms and the atmosphere surrounding them gradually increased the accuracy of the predicted storm tracks and also the times they were expected to make landfall. Special weather satellites, plus reconnaissance aircraft equipped with the latest scientific measuring equipment and the precise

Hurricane Katrina is about to go ashore along the Gulf Coast in August 2005. *NOAA photo.*

navigation capabilities of GPS, all combine to provide accurate, timely location, and real-time intensity data.

The computers used today for weather forecasting are no different from any others in at least one respect: garbage in, garbage out. They are just bigger, faster, and capable of processing vastly more data at much higher speeds than our familiar desktop models. But if the information being processed is flawed, the results will be too. However, the far more precise information being input today makes a huge difference. Whereas it was once extremely difficult to forecast storm movement even 24 hours in advance, the predictive models now in use are capable of delivering very good forecasts, often as much as three or four days in advance and sometimes even longer than that.

Unfortunately, intensity predictions have not yet become as dependable as location forecasts, especially where explosive strengthening is concerned. There are a few numerical models designed for this, but at best they are still a work in progress. New predictive models are constantly under development; thus there is little doubt in my mind that eventually we will have determined enough of the necessary input parameters to make intensity forecasts much more reliable.

Staying Informed

If you live anywhere in the United States that is susceptible to hurricane damage, and if a hurricane or tropical storm is threatening your area, in today's world you will be unable to avoid being bombarded by the latest information. You'll hear it on local radio stations, and you most certainly will see it at home on all of your local television stations. Another source is one of the many makes of battery-operated NOAA weather radios.

Watching on-scene TV hurricane coverage can become addictive. Reporters appear on camera from various locations in the threatened area or even during actual landfall, some of them foolishly standing right out in the open while being buffeted by high winds. They seem oblivious to the fact that it is not the wind itself that kills, but rather the "missile hazard" of airborne debris that has in at least a few cases even caused decapitation. This practice invites disaster, and sooner or later I fear something really bad is going to happen in real time to one of those reporters while on scene, right in front of the camera.

But if you can tear yourself away from this sensationalist and often pointless coverage and stick to the important facts, you'll be far better able to make the necessary preparations to weather the oncoming storm.

Most coastal TV stations have at least one trained meteorologist on staff. The larger stations may even have a team of qualified weather experts. The important thing is that these folks tend to stick to the facts and avoid unnecessary speculation.

Most of the stations either have their own radar, or are linked to a nearby NOAA weather station's radar. Plus there is a plethora of weather information in the Internet that includes live radar and satellite imagery as

As of 1800 UTC (1PM CDT), Hurricane Katrina was located 180 mi (290km) SSE of the mouth of the Mississippi River and was moving NW at 13 MPH (21 KPH).

Maximum sustained winds were 175 MPH (282KPH) making Katrina a category 5 storm on the Saffir-Simpson scale.

Credit: NOAA

NOAA -17 RGB= CH(1,1,4) 08/28/2005 16:47 UTC

Satellite image of Hurricane Katrina in the Gulf of Mexico just south of New Orleans on August 28, 2005. Katrina was a Category 5 storm at the time. *NOAA photo.*

well as the current watches and warnings. A list of some of these websites appears at the end of this chapter.

How the Forecasts Are Made

Even with weather satellites and high-speed computers, experience still counts a great deal. That's why NOAA staffs its National Hurricane Center in Miami with the best human forecasters available. And, thanks to the necessary funding, we now have a wide variety of meteorological information sources. Special weather satellites monitor the tropics 24 hours per day, constantly sending back both visible and infrared imagery of what's going on in the areas where hurricanes form.

Many commercial and almost all military ships at sea send detailed weather information every six hours, a tradition that goes back to the early days of radio-telephones. Some of these surface vessels are even equipped to send balloon-borne equipment into the upper atmosphere to obtain critical data.

Once something suspicious (nowadays labeled an "area of interest") appears on a satellite image, or is determined through analysis of ship weather data, it is closely monitored for any significant changes. If it reaches the stage of consideration for tropical development, it is declared an area to be investigated, and if it shows any potential for serious development, a Hurricane Hunter aircraft is launched to check it out.

When it is determined to be a tropical depression, it gets the next available number in sequence for the current hurricane season, and predictive mathematical computer models are run. There are currently at least 10 such models designed to forecast the track of a storm. Some are used as stand-alone systems, and some are used collectively in groups called ensembles.

These models use both current observations and statistical data to predict future movement. Observing hurricanes movement tend to move much like watching a leaf floating around on a stream, and trying to predict where it will be at any given time in the future by analyzing the somewhat divergent air currents that carry it along. The accuracy of forecasting of that leaf's future location is determined by how well our model can predict the future movements of those currents themselves.

Close-up satellite image of Hurricane Katrina in the Gulf of Mexico just south of New Orleans on August 28, 2005. *NOAA photo.*

Just how well these predictive models work in the world of tropical storms and hurricanes also depends on the intensity of the storms. A weak depression has less effect on the surrounding atmosphere than a major hurricane, which typically results in conflicting forecasts generated by various models. But as a rule forecast tracks become increasingly more accurate as the storm grows stronger.

In the majority of cases, forecasters run most—if not all—of the available models at almost the same time. And, as you'd expect, 10 different models will produce 10 (at least somewhat) different forecast tracks. As mentioned above, a very weak depression will often generate models in great disagreement, while for a strong storm embedded in a well-defined atmospheric current flow, nearly all of the models will usually be in close agreement.

Experience Still Counts!

When the models scatter the predicted future locations all over the map, which one (if any) is considered the most reliable? This is where human experience really counts. Years of detailed records for each model indicate the atmospheric conditions under which each performed most reliably. This knowledge, combined with the human forecaster's own years of tropical storm and hurricane experience, becomes the basis for the official track forecast.

Then there is the matter of predicted intensity. Being able to predict precisely when and where a hurricane will go ashore, as well as how large and how strong its winds will be, is the ultimate goal of the forecast system. The more advanced the warning the affected area receives, the better it can prepare. Fewer lives will be lost, and structural damage can be prevented as much as possible under the circumstances.

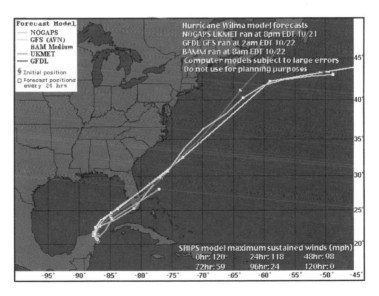

Hurricane Wilma computer forecasts. *NOAA photo.*

Infrared satellite image of Hurricane Rita in the Gulf of Mexico, September, 2005. Rita was a Category 5 storm with 180 mph winds at this time, but fortunately had decreased to a Category 3 with 125 mph winds by the time it made landfall. *NOAA photo.*

Internet Sources of Tropical Weather Information

There are numerous sources of good, up-to-date tropical weather information on the Internet—too many to list here. You can find others yourself if you use Google, Yahoo, or another search engine to look for them by simply typing in "tropical weather." Among the many you will see are some of my own favorites:

www.crownweather.com/tropical.html—I especially like this one because it offers such a great amount of information, charts, and other graphics that include outstanding satellite imagery. Included are all the various forecasts, computer models, hurricane tracks, tropical weather outlooks and discussions, upper air charts, and much, much more. The last page of this website also has a long list of valuable Internet links that take you to additional websites, such as Hurricane Alley, Early Alert, HurricaneTrack.com, and many more. Definitely worth the visit, regardless of whether you are a tropical weather buff or simply want to know a little more about the subject.

www.nhc.noaa.gov—All of the tropical weather information currently available is offered on this website, including historic information of past storms. I don't find it quite as well organized for easy day-to-day use as Crown Weather, but it is all there if you are willing to dig a little for it. Another good government website is *www.srh.noaa.gov*/tropicalwx, which also offers tracking maps you can download and print. Another good tracking map for the western Atlantic is located at *www .nhc.noaa.gov/AT_Track_chart2.pdf*.

www.wunderground.com/tropical—Yet another good website for tropical information, not quite as rich in detailed current information as Crown Weather, but it also does offer excellent, well-organized historical archives of past Atlantic basin hurricanes going back all the way to 1851.

www.weather.com/newscenter/tropical—This is a good website for tropical weather information, with lots of good satellite imagery.

El Niño and La Niña information: There are a number of websites that offer detailed information about this unique tropical Pacific phenomenon, including an explanation of what it is, how it forms, the effects it has on global weather, and analysis of the current El Niño or La Niña conditions. One of my own favorites is the NOAA El Niño Page, found at *www.elnino.noaa.gov*.

www.hurricanealley.net/hurrevac.htm—This website offers hurricane evacuation information. I have not verified any of this information through my own use, so be sure to check out any references to your area for accuracy.

CHAPTER 5
Understanding Watches and Warnings

If you live in an area under the threat of a hurricane or tropical storm, the most prudent policy is to prepare for the worst and hope for the best. If the storm isn't as bad when it finally arrives as the warnings indicated, be happy—not mad at the forecasters. After all, they are charged with the responsibility of keeping you as safe as possible. And if it turns out to be worse than expected, just be pleased you were wise enough to have done your best to be properly prepared.

Hurricane forecasting has improved dramatically over the past few decades, and as accurate as the track predictions are today, they still aren't perfect. Sometimes a hurricane doesn't go ashore precisely where predicted. That's why a cone of error always surrounds the forecast track. As you can see by the illustration showing a forecast for Hurricane Wilma in 2005, that cone becomes wider with time—much wider at the 72-hour forecast point than the 48-hour forecast point, which is wider than at the 24-hour point, and so on.

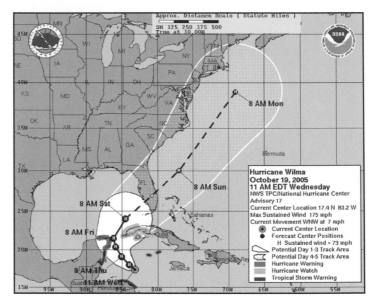

Hurricane Wilma 5-day official forecast. *NOAA photo.*

And that's precisely why you should never focus on the thin black line as a precise point of landfall. For example, the skinny black line that forecast the 24-hour landfall of Hurricane Charley (a Category 4) in August of 2004 actually intersected the coastline near the Tampa, Florida area. However, Charley veered slightly to the right and marched up Charlotte Harbor just north of Fort Myers—still well within the cone of error. Unfortunately too many residents of that area depended entirely on the thin black line and ignored the forecast cone of error with disastrous consequences. Nevertheless they were quick to blame the forecasters for not providing adequate warning.

Most hurricanes will have a strong hurricane-force wind field that extends many miles on both sides of its actual track. Some of these dangerous wind fields may be only 25 miles wide, while others are more than 100 miles. Hurricane Wilma in October 2005, for example, was a real monster; it came ashore in southwest Florida near Everglades City as a Category 3 and crossed the state on a northeast heading. It was so large that

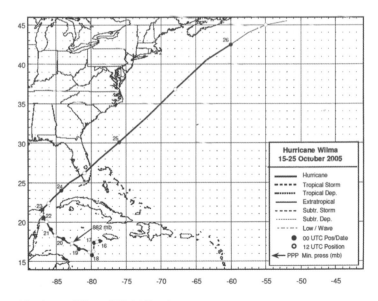

Hurricane Wilma Official Track. *NOAA photo.*

hurricane force winds were experienced over a swath almost 200 miles wide that crossed the entire peninsula from southwest to northeast. My point is that even if you are over 100 miles away on either side of the forecast storm track, never assume you will be completely safe.

Hurricane Warnings

Hurricane and tropical storm watches and warnings are posted by the National Hurricane Center at six-hour intervals (5:00 and 11:00 a.m. and p.m., EDT, in the Eastern Time Zone, 4:00 and 10:00 a.m. and p.m., EDT, in the Central Time Zone). As the storm gets closer to landfall, intermediate advisories are also posted at two- or three-hour intervals in between the standard warning times, depending upon the proximity and intensity of the storm.

A ***hurricane watch*** is issued for your area when there is a good possibility that you could experience hurricane conditions (winds of 74 mph or greater) within 36 hours. Such advisories are almost always issued for any location within the forecast track cone of error at that time. By now you should be seriously considering making the necessary preparations.

A ***hurricane warning*** means that sustained winds of 74 mph or greater are expected in your area within 24 hours. At this point you are taking a great risk if you have not already started to get prepared. And if you are in a flood zone where evacuation is indicated, you should be at least completely ready to go—or better yet, already on the way.

Hurricane and tropical storm warnings are issued in the following formats:

Public Advisory—Issued in text format to be read over radios (including NOAA weather radios) and TV; it contains information on all watches and warnings being issued at that time, the storm's current location, predicted storm movement, wind and central pressure, and the time of the next advisory.

Forecast/Advisory—This was formerly known as the Marine Advisory. It contains all of the information contained in the Public Advisory, plus an eye size estimate, maximum sustained wind, wind radii, and some wave height information, as well as forecasts for the storm's future 12-, 24-, 36-, 48-,72-, 96-, and 120-hour storm positions.

Forecast Track—This is the graphic image you see on TV during any discussion of an existing hurricane or tropical storm. You can also view these images via many Internet tropical weather sites, including those listed in Chapter 4.

Tropical Weather Outlook—Issued twice daily at 11:00 a.m. and p.m., EDT, during the hurricane season from June 1 through November 30. This brief message simply states the forecaster's outlook for potential tropical storm or hurricane development over the next 24 to

48 hours. It is often read on radio and TV stations, as well as being available over the Internet.

Don't Wait For Landfall

If you have not completed all preparations well before the eye of the storm reaches your area, you have waited too long. A large major hurricane can start producing hurricane-force winds and coastal storm surge flooding in your area many hours before the center gets there. So, figure that when the storm is forecast to arrive in 24 hours, you actually have no more than 12 hours, as the absolute maximum, before the first strong winds from the storm begin to reach your area. And even then you should already have completed all outside preparations that would be difficult in a strong wind. And remember, *never* expect the hurricane to precisely follow the skinny black line on the forecast map. If you are anywhere within the 24-hour forecast cone of error, you had better have all preparations completed as soon as possible.

It is very difficult to handle large objects even in winds of only 30 mph, especially large sheets of plywood and metal storm panels. Although the metal panels do not have particularly sharp edges, when they are being pushed forcibly by strong winds they can do very serious damage to anything in the area—especially the human body.

Driving any vehicle is also difficult; it only gets worse as the wind increases, and the probability of a rollover accident increases considerably. Lighter vehicles are even more at risk. That's why you want to be completely ready well before the storm center arrives. Inadequate preparation (see Chapters 7 and 8) can easily lead to serious, sometimes life-threatening injuries, and you cannot expect an emergency medical response team on your doorstep until the winds subside to less than 45 mph after the center of the storm has passed. If the storm is large and slow moving, this could take many hours. In extreme situations, it could be a day or even more! It is not unprecedented for a major hurricane to stall and remain in one location for more than 24 hours.

CHAPTER 6
Damage Hurricanes Do and Why

By far the most damage done by hurricanes and tropical storms — up to 80 percent by some estimates — is caused by water, which comes from two sources: rain and storm surge along the coast. If you live inland, especially near any sort of waterway (river, lake, canal) or in a low-lying area, your biggest worry is rain-induced flooding. If you live on or near the coast, a wind-borne surge of seawater can penetrate many miles inland, depending upon the strength of the wind, the height of the surge, and the geography of the area.

Many hurricanes are extremely "wet," bringing with them huge amounts of rain — up to 20 inches (or more, in extreme situations) in a single day. And if the storm moves slowly, the rain has a chance to build up over a relatively large area, an effect that can extend even hundreds of miles inland. So while 20 inches of rain may not sound like much to those of who have never experienced a flood, keep in mind that water always runs downhill and the lower elevations inevitably get the

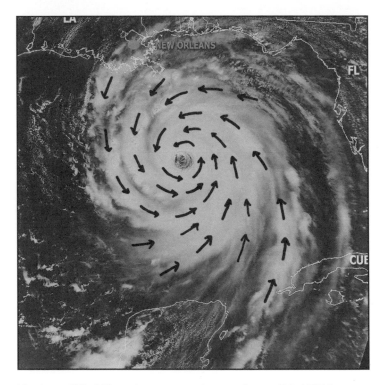

Hurricane Wind Flow: Arrows superimposed upon this NOAA satellite image of Hurricane Katrina (August 2005) show how air moves in a converging pattern into the storm.

worst of it. Most municipalities issue maps of their areas showing flood potential. You should be aware of how vulnerable your location is, and whether or not you need flood insurance.

Even tropical storms can dump massive amounts of rain hundreds of miles inland, especially if they are large and slow moving. This can be a common problem when any hurricane, large or small, moves inland and downgrades into a tropical storm or sometimes even a depression. The wind may no longer be a threat, but the rain still has the potential to cause flooding of disastrous proportions.

On the other hand, some hurricanes are considered "dry" because they bring little rain with them and move through rapidly. These are the storms that cause most of their damage via wind, as well as storm surge along coastal areas.

Storm Surge

Storm surge is caused by the extremely high-velocity onshore winds on the right side of the hurricane's track that push a massive wall of water directly against a section of coast. In a hurricane moving from east to west, the storm surge will be caused by the winds in the northern semicircle—the half of the storm that's north of the eye. For a storm approaching the west coast of Florida and thus moving from west to east, the storm surge will occur on the south side of the eye (the southern semicircle). The stronger the winds, the higher the storm surge. In a Category 4 or 5 storm, this surge can exceed 20 feet. And if it coincides with high tide, it is obviously going to be that much higher.

Add to this the often huge waves that accompany the surge, and the damage potential skyrockets.

Massive beach erosion is a certainty, and if there are buildings close to the water's edge they are at risk of disappearing completely. In low, flat coastal areas like western Louisiana, surge damage can extend inland for a great distance, as it did in Hurricane Rita in 2005 when the surge severely damaged or destroyed buildings many miles inland.

Flooding

A wet tropical storm or hurricane can dump a huge amount of rain over a large area in a short amount of time. As this water drains into the lowest area, it accumulates rapidly and flooding begins. Houses located in this area are at risk as the water rises, high enough to reach the ceiling in some cases. Rainwater runoff also dumps into rivers, which quickly rise to dangerous flood stage with fast currents strong enough to move an entire house. Sometimes there are more deaths this way than from coastal storm surge. Lakes get deeper and consequently larger, covering even more of the surrounding area and thereby flooding nearby houses.

Wind Damage

The force of the wind alone in a strong hurricane can do a lot of damage. An increase in wind force is not proportional to an increase in wind speed. If the wind

Massive flooding in New Orleans by Hurricane Katrina, August 2005. *NOAA photo.*

velocity doubles, the force it produces is almost four times greater. That's one of many reasons why a Category 4 storm with 140 mph winds is enormously more destructive than a Category 1 with only 75 mph winds.

Don't think that if you live high up in a tall building that you are any safer from wind damage. The wind speeds listed in hurricane warnings are based upon measurements approximately 10 feet above ground level. But a 140 mph wind at ground level becomes 165 mph (or more) just 100 feet higher because there is little of the friction effect that reduces wind speed at ground level.

And by the way—contrary to popular belief that it is the overall difference in atmospheric air pressure between outside, in the storm, and inside your house that lifts the roof off—that difference is actually very small. However, if one or more large windows get blown in, then the force of the wind can increase the pressure inside your house sufficiently to cause a weak or poorly anchored roof to fail. So forget the idea of keeping a window on the downwind side of the house partially

Damage in Mississippi by Hurricane Katrina in 2005.
FEMA photo by Marty Bahamonde.

A flat roof's covering weakened by age is no match for hurricane winds. *Photo by author.*

open "to relieve air pressure," and by all means keep every one of them tightly shut (doors, too) and safely shuttered until the storm has passed.

Missile Hazards

Anything that is not too heavy for the wind to move has the potential to become an airborne missile. Tree limbs, boards, and discarded trash are especially likely to fly in strong winds, frequently at high enough velocities to be extremely dangerous. More human and animal injuries are caused by flying debris than by wind alone, as well as structural damage. Automobile windows are especially vulnerable.

During Hurricane Andrew (Miami, 1992), a friend of mine had a very close call when a sharp-edged fist-size piece of barrel tile from a nearby roof exploded through an un-shuttered window, missing him by just inches, and buried itself in a wall so deeply that it took a pry bar and some serious digging to extract it. He told me afterward that he doubted he would have survived a head or upper body hit by that missile—especially if he had to wait hours before medical help arrived, which would have likely been the case.

Several obvious lessons here: Don't stay in a room with windows, if at all possible. Or, at the very least, have all windows protected by code-approved shutters strong enough to keep stuff like that outside where it belongs. And by all means clear your yard of any loose items that might become airborne in a hurricane. Encourage your neighbors to do the same.

Rain

Other than contributing to flooding, rain by itself would not be an unusual problem were it not for the wind, which drives it almost horizontally with such great force that it gets rain through any crack or crevice in your house. Windows not sealed properly or protected by storm shutters are especially vulnerable to water intrusion caused by the very force of wind pressure. And if flying debris breaks any glass, the problem instantly becomes far worse.

One of the most common structural wind-related problems in a strong hurricane is roof damage. This is often not the complete removal of the roof, but rather the systematic destruction of the materials that make up the roof covering. Once this occurs the roof is no longer watertight and a large amount of rainwater gets inside the house and the trouble begins.

More houses suffer from this type of damage than anything else, as evidenced by the vast number of large plastic tarpaulins that quickly appear after a big storm. But it is physically impossible to put a tarp on your roof during a storm, and that's when the worst damage often occurs. Interior flooding can do irreparable damage to carpets, drapes, furniture, appliances, and everything else that should not get wet. Cleanup of this horrible mess is time-consuming, and disheartening. The total bill often adds up to far more than just the roof repair, or even the cost of a completely new roof, all of which suddenly just got a lot more expensive than it would have been before the storm.

Inside the Storm

Nothing is constant inside a strong hurricane except an all-encompassing, enervating state of fear and apprehension. The winds change direction as the storm moves past your location, rising and falling like

Blue plastic tarps cover roofs damaged by Hurricane Charley (2004) in Florida. *FEMA photo by Mark Wolfe.*

the shrieking furies from hell. The gusts are especially terrifying, rapidly rising to a screaming pitch that makes your hair stand on end as they go up the scale to maximum velocity and then subside again. The force of these gusts slams against the sides of your house like a giant sledgehammer. Flying debris bangs deafeningly against walls and window shutters like the rattle of a machine gun, penetrating anything not strong enough to withstand its forceful impact.

This is no time to even think about going outside. Stay away from windows and doors; go as deeply into the strongest part of the house as possible, even if it is a closet or a bathroom. Many fortunate survivors have beat the odds during the worst of hurricanes by climbing into the bathtub or a closet and covering themselves with a mattress. A friend of mine and his wife managed to get through Hurricane Andrew without injury by using a mattress to cover themselves while lying down inside a small boat on a trailer in the garage as the storm proceeded to systematically destroy their house around them.

Mobile homes are especially vulnerable to high winds because of their thin walls and light overall construction. The way they selectively get destroyed by a strong hurricane defied explanation, until recently. In any trailer park during a big storm, some structures will survive almost unscathed, while others right next to them are totally blown to bits. Meteorologists have recently determined that this seemingly random selection of what stays and what goes is the result of very narrow, super-strong gusty bands of wind called microbursts. In a hurricane with sustained winds of 100 mph, for example, a microburst can hit 200 mph or more with tornado-like effects. These short-lived microbursts occur randomly within the strongest portion of the storm's wind field, which is the area surrounding the eye, referred to as the eye wall.

There is serious danger, too, in the outer part of the storm. In some hurricanes there are even occasional tornados, and frequently severe thunderstorms. So never

Hurricane Charley (2004) mobile home damage in Florida. *FEMA photo by Andrea Booher.*

assume that just because the strongest winds have passed the storm is over. And don't forget the calm in the eye of the storm if it happens to come your way; it will last for only a few minutes before the high winds suddenly return, often stronger than before.

I cannot stress strongly enough how important it is that windows must be protected by strong shutters (see Chapter 9). Placing masking tape on the glass is complete waste of time (also difficult to remove afterward) and offers absolutely no protection. Only code-approved shutters or heavy plywood (5/8- to 3/4-inch) will do. The strongest and by far the most wind resistant and rainproof doors are out-opening, because they are backed by a frame along all edges. If you have any in-opening doors (the double-door variety are the weakest), by all means protect them with outside code-approved shutters.

And be patient. Unless absolutely forced to evacuate, your odds of survival are far better if you stay inside until the hurricane is completely past.

Damage Prevention Through Research

Although research into prevention and reduction of hurricane damage has been ongoing for decades, efforts have been amplified dramatically in recent years.

Until recently one of the biggest obstacles in such research was developing the laboratory tools necessary to determine the effects of hurricane-force wind and rain on building materials before they are used in actual construction, which otherwise would mean having to wait until a major hurricane actually came along to put these materials to the test. And of course that could mean years of waiting, if it ever happened at all. All too often in past decades, materials and techniques that had been in use for years because in theory they were hurricane-proof have proved not as good as they were originally thought to be.

By the year 2005 that began to change, as laboratory tools were developed to accurately simulate the damaging effects of a major hurricane, so that materials and techniques could be tested and developed before being implemented in building construction. One of the first such tools was the air cannon, developed by Tim Reinhold at the International Hurricane Research Center in Miami, Florida.

The concept is simple enough: Basically it's a section of heavy-wall PVC pipe large enough in diameter and long enough to hold an eight-foot 2x4. High-pressure air is used to fire this piece of wood end-first at 52 mph, about the same speed it would attain if airborne in a Category 5 hurricane. If the 2x4 penetrates the object it is fired at, that structure is deemed not strong enough to safely resist flying debris in a major hurricane.

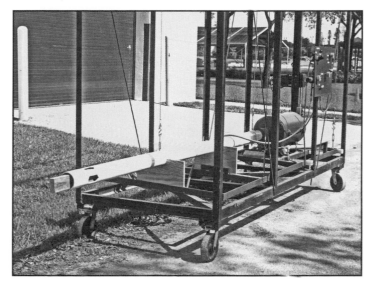

This is the air cannon developed by the International Hurricane Research Center. It is used to fire an 8-foot long piece of 2x4-inch lumber at hurricane wind speeds. *IRHC Photo.*

Believe it or not, that flying 2x4 will even penetrate concrete if it is not of proper thickness and strength. And it does not even slow down if it hits a window that is not protected with heavy plywood or code-approved shutters. For that reason Miami-Dade County in Florida has adopted the results of the air-cannon testing program in their building codes, a huge step up in damage prevention.

But, what about the direct effects of high velocity wind and rain alone? In 2007 the University of Florida built a machine to simulate a Category 3 hurricane with winds of 130 mph. This is a huge fan system powered by four marine diesel engines that also incorporates water jets to produce wind-driven rain at up to 35 inches per hour. It is large enough to test an entire house at once, thus enabling engineers to determine the overall effect of wind and rain in real time on the walls, windows, roof, doors, and all other elements of construction.

So far researchers have been using the system to test vacant homes for hurricane readiness and to develop recommendations for new building standards.

As of yet no one has developed a laboratory machine to duplicate storm surge and flooding, and certainly such equipment would be extremely costly to build. But perhaps that is not even necessary; there are plenty of storm surge and flood events around the United States and other countries with coastal areas vulnerable to hurricane impact, which provide ongoing opportunities to study these problems in depth. After all, storm surge damage is primarily an effect of location.

And sadly, in many areas the potential for storm surge damage is steadily increasing every year as we continue to develop more and more of our fragile coastlines. Such development also extends the probability that storm surges will reach much farther inland because of this elimination of critical naturally occurring buffer zones.

Hurricane Wind Machine: This machine is large enough and strong enough to blow a poorly built house to pieces. *Photo by Jimmy Jesteadt, Department of Civil and Coastal Engineering, University of Florida.*

CHAPTER 7
The List

Year after year, whenever there is a hurricane threat anywhere along the coastal United States, I see exactly the same scenario on the TV news a day or so before the expected landfall. There's a frantic last-minute rush on local hardware stores and lumberyards for materials to protect windows, and similar panic at local grocery stores to stock up on food. Critical items, like plywood or storm panels to cover windows, quickly become in short supply. Tempers flare, the roads are clogged, and the auto accident rate goes up. Often the weather is already beginning to deteriorate, which further aggravates a bad situation.

Then after the storm begins the aftermath. Those of us who have been through a major hurricane or two already know what that is like. Total chaos is the order of the day: food, ice, gasoline, and other commodities we are accustomed to buying routinely are not readily available, if in fact they're available at all. Some critical items may not be obtainable for days. Supermarkets that have lost electrical power have no way to protect perishables, thus eliminating another source of food. Gas stations without power may have plenty of fuel in their underground tanks, but no way to pump it into your automobile.

The situation almost always continues to worsen for at least a few days. I'm always amazed by how quickly— often within an hour or two—after the storm passes there are suddenly long lines of unfortunates who must now stand in the hot sun and passing rain showers for hours to get a few bottles of drinking water and perhaps a bag or two of ice, which are being handed out for free by federal, state, or county emergency services. If these individuals had prepared properly before the storm, they certainly would not have to be there. Plus, the expense and manpower now required to provide these supplies could certainly be better utilized in other, more critical post-storm rescue operations.

The scenario following a major hurricane is often worse than a Hollywood horror movie. Some areas of Miami after Hurricane Andrew in 1992 and again in Louisiana and Mississippi after Hurricane Katrina in 2005 looked much like the aftermath of a nuclear bomb detonation. Damage was widespread and defied description: trees and power lines were down, roads were blocked or flooded. Houses were completely demolished. Rarely could you find a store or anything else open for days.

Most road signs were gone, and the world was changed so dramatically it was hard to tell where you were, even if you'd lived there all of your life.

This is definitely *not* a safe time to be out wandering around looking for those items you failed to buy before the storm came. Below is my list of those basic items every household should have on hand well before the storm gets there.

Hurricane Checklist

At the beginning of each hurricane season, I make up a checklist to remind me, or anyone else who might have to act in my absence, of all the steps necessary to prepare for an approaching storm. Here are the most important items on my list:

- Verify homeowners', windstorm, and flood insurance policies are up to date and stored in a safe, dry place where you can get to them immediately after the storm.
- Make a list of necessary medications and keep sufficient quantities on hand to ensure you have enough to last for at least a week (better yet, two weeks).
- Put up storm shutters (be sure you know where necessary hardware and tools are located).

- Stock up on containers to be filled with water for drinking.

- Fill the bathtub with water (make sure the stopper is watertight).

- Set refrigerator and freezer controls as cold as possible, at least 24 hours before forecast landfall.

- Secure or store any loose items that can blow around and cause damage.

- Park the family auto in a safe place with windows tightly closed.

- Check supplies of food, water, ice, and other items needed to survive after the storm.

- Inventory flashlights and have plenty of extra batteries.

- Assemble a battery-powered radio, and maybe also a battery-powered TV.

- Locate any special bracing to be installed, such as for the garage door or fence gates.

- Remove TV antenna or satellite dish if deemed necessary, but be wary of nearby power lines while doing this.

- Review your evacuation route, which should already be mapped out if you live on or near the coast where storm surge is a threat, or even inland where flooding is possible.

- Assemble any other personal items you do not want to be without.

Make the list as comprehensive as possible to fit your own situation in order to avoid overlooking something important in the haste of storm preparation.

Water

After the storm, it may not be safe to drink tap water, even if it is still available. A pressure loss in the water distribution network of delivery pipes enhances the risk of bacteria contamination. So either stock up on bottled water or keep large, clean containers on hand that you can fill before the storm comes. Figure on a gallon per day for each person.

I prefer to go the storage container route. We routinely save large plastic jugs that juice and other beverages come in. Once empty, we wash and thoroughly dry them, then store them in large plastic garbage bags where they are out of the way until needed.

Since water may also be needed for flushing toilets and other hygiene, I keep a half-dozen inexpensive plastic trash containers, with lids, nested inside each other. The five-gallon size is good for this, since they are easy to handle and store. A bathtub as full of water as you can safely fill it, with a bucket handy nearby, is also

Filling five-gallon plastic trash cans with water that can be used for washing and flushing toilets if necessary. *Photo by author.*

useful for flushing toilets, but not safe for drinking. Make sure the stopper doesn't leak.

Tap water should be considered unsafe after a storm until you have officially been informed otherwise, simply because you have no way of knowing if there was a pressure drop somewhere in the system. But that does not mean you cannot drink it if it still runs clear, and if you take the following steps to purify it. Keep a small bottle of laundry bleach (I use Clorox) on hand and add 15 drops per gallon of water. Shake well, and let

Adding laundry bleach to water to make it safe to drink.
Photo by author.

stand for 30 minutes before drinking. Surprisingly, there is very little taste of chlorine in the water. *Do not* use this method with any outside standing water; the dangerous bacteria load is potentially far too high to be completely eliminated this way. Don't try this with any water that is not completely clear unless you have a safe way to filter it before treating it.

Refrigeration

At least 24 hours before the hurricane's forecasted landfall, you should have turned the freezer and refrigerator temperature controls as low as they can go. Remember, it's possible to lose power long before the most intense part of the storm reaches your area.

If you have space in your freezer, set it to its lowest temperature and fill all available space with containers full of water to make ice (leave a little air space at the top of each container to accommodate the expansion of water as it freezes). Do this at least 24 to 36 hours in advance, if at all possible. And if you have a well-insulated ice chest, buy block ice (which keeps much longer than crushed ice) a day or two before. Try to completely fill it and leave it tightly shut until you actually need it. Ice will be usable for three to four days this way, if you are careful.

Food in the freezer will keep for up to three days after power goes out—even though it will likely begin to thaw in 36 to 48 hours, but only if the door is opened no more than absolutely necessary. Open the refrigerator door as little as possible. It should hold the cold well enough for food to stay good up to 24 hours before it begins to spoil.

By the way, a small generator can provide enough electrical power to keep a refrigerator and even another freezer cold enough to protect the contents (see Chapter 11).

Food

Keep enough canned food on hand for at least four or five days. A full week is even better.

Lighting

There are two types of battery-powered lights that have worked well for me. To provide light for a room, I like fluorescent hand lanterns that operate on standard C or D cells. Stay away from anything that requires unusual or difficult-to-find batteries or bulbs. Fluorescent lights last many, many hours, but it's still a good idea to keep enough spare batteries on hand to reload them completely at least twice.

One of the great recent advances in flashlights is the super bright Light Emitting Diode (LED). For the same amount of light as the typical incandescent bulb, standard AAA, AA, C, and D batteries will last 10 to 20 times longer. LED flashlights initially cost a little more than the standard variety, but the payback occurs after only two or three battery replacements. And the LEDs themselves typically last 50,000 to 100,000 hours.

Try to stay away from candles and any other open flames as sources of light. They have a terrible track

Useful lights when the power is out. The hand lantern at left puts out a strong beam that covers more distance, but it also uses batteries rapidly. The batteries in the LED flashlight in the middle will last up to 10 times longer than a standard flashlight, and about 4 times longer in the fluorescent lantern on the right. *Photo by author.*

record when it comes to starting fires; why go through all the trouble to protect your home from the storm only to burn it down afterwards?

Waterproofing

Sensitive items, such as computers, TVs, and expensive or antique furniture can be protected from leaky roofs with large plastic garbage bags and cheap plastic tarpaulins. Even tarps large enough to cover much of your roof cost very little. I keep several on hand at all times, because they can also be used to cover the roof temporarily after the storm passes, and you may have to wait months for permanent roof repairs. (See Chapter 9 for more information on roof tarps.)

Keeping Cool

I keep one small 12-volt auto-type fan on hand for each bedroom. A small battery of the type used for compact cars, electric-start riding lawnmowers, or motorcycles will power one of these fans all night for up to two or three nights (depending upon the battery's capacity) before recharging is necessary. Make sure the battery is fully charged before the storm arrives. An inexpensive 12-volt battery charger is perfect for this, and can also be used with a generator.

An inexpensive 12V car fan clip-mounted on the edge of an open container with a battery inside the container makes an efficient portable cooling system when the power is out.

Photo by author.

Clothing and Bedding

Keep at least one change of clothing and bed coverings in a dry place. Large plastic garbage bags are good for this. Ditto for pillows, sleeping bags, and similar items.

Keeping Up with What's Going On

A battery-powered AM/FM radio is my first choice. I also keep a NOAA weather radio on hand in case local radio and TV stations go out, but frankly the information on these radios is not updated or detailed enough to suit me. You can also add a small black-and-white 12-volt TV to the list, if you want. They are not expensive. But, keep in mind that as of June 2009 the TV broadcast industry stopped transmitting the old-style analog signals, rendering older TVs inoperative without cable service or a converter box. Analog-to-digital converters are available for older TVs, but they require 110-volt AC to work. Look for newer portables that are digital-ready, if you want to use TV while the electrical power is out. In any case, don't skip the battery-powered AM/FM radio in favor of the TV; it's possible that the storm may knock out all TV stations within range while at least a few radio stations are still transmitting.

If you have a cellular telephone, make sure it is completely charged before the storm arrives. And don't use it for idle conversation after the storm; it may have to last many days before your hard-wired household telephone is back in service.

Gasoline for Your Car

Gas may not be available for days, so try to fill the tank before the storm and stay off the road as much as possible.

It is my habit throughout the entire hurricane season to keep the tank at least half-filled at all times.

If you did your due diligence before the storm, except for an unforeseen emergency, there should be no reason to leave home for at least three or four days. The road system will be a mess anyway, so don't become part of it. Besides, staying at home is a good way to prevent looting by those who failed to prepare properly.

CHAPTER 8
Should You Evacuate?

The closer you are to the coast, the more likely it is that you will be in an evacuation zone. And if you are located in one of these zones, it is important that you note which particular one you are in. And by the way, your designated evacuation zone may not necessarily match the particular storm surge zone you are in.

Confused? The only thing that really counts is whether you should evacuate or not. So pay close attention to official statements issued by government agencies in your area. And if evacuation is recommended for your location, pay particular attention to whether is it simply a recommendation, or mandatory. Mandatory is definitely more serious, typically issued as a command or direct order when it is felt that your area is dangerously susceptible to flooding or storm surge. Whether or not you leave is ultimately up to you, but if the evacuation is mandatory there will usually be a police presence in your area asking you to leave.

Typically, for safety reasons, officials usually issue evacuations for one or sometimes even two storm categories higher than what they are expecting at that time. For example, if there is a Category 1 hurricane approaching, but you live in a Category 3 evacuation zone, you may still be asked to leave, due to uncertainties associated with the storm track and the possibility of a sudden significant increase in intensity before it arrives.

The type of building you live in has a lot to do with whether or not you should evacuate. House trailers and manufactured homes are especially at risk because of their light construction. So take those items you feel are most important, and leave.

While some states use maps of storm surge zones as a guide, it is more common to use easily recognizable roadways such as interstates and highways to determine evacuation zones. For example, if you live on the East Coast of the United States and your house is on the east side of U.S. Highway 1, or Interstate 95, you could be asked to get out.

Storm surge maps for your area are available online. You can find them the same way I did, by searching Google or Yahoo with the term "hurricane storm surge maps." Florida's, for example, are located at *www .floridadisaster.org/publicmapping/index.htm*.

Hurricane evacuation route sign. *Photo by author.*

Double-Edged Sword

Probably some of the most chilling scenes on the evening news during the exceptionally violent hurricane season of 2005 were endless lines of gridlocked autos on roads leading away from the coast. There have even been instances where the potential for human casualties was greater along a jammed evacuation route than it would have been for people who simply stayed home.

So, should you never evacuate? Of course not. But there are ways to avoid getting caught up in a dangerous traffic jam where you could be overtaken by the approaching storm you are so desperately trying to run away from.

First and foremost: *Do not wait until the last minute*. Button up your house and secure everything valuable as best you can and hit the road at least 24 hours before predicted landfall. A 36- or 48-hour head start is even better. And make sure you have a full tank of gas before you go; if you wait until the last minute to gas up, you may be caught in hours-long lines at the gas station. And be sure to take those items with you that are critical. The Red Cross has an excellent Hurricane Evacuation Checklist for just this purpose. You can find it on their website at *www.redcross.org/static/file_cont4470_lang0_1577.pdf*.

Included in the suggested items are:

- Maps
- Non-perishable or canned food
- Can opener (non-electric)
- Bottled water
- Clothing
- Rainwear
- Bedding
- Sleeping bags
- Pillows
- Battery-operated radio
- Flashlight
- Extra batteries
- Prescriptions and medications
- First-aid kit

Special items for:

- Infants
- Elderly
- People with disabilities

Important documents (in a waterproof container):

- Driver's license

- Social Security card
- Proof of residence
- Insurance policies
- Tax records
- Birth and marriage certificates

Obviously the family auto could be filled to capacity, depending upon the number of individuals aboard and the gear needed. If you just do not have room for everything, carefully sort out those items you can leave behind and store them where they will remain safe and dry until your return.

One of the most difficult areas to evacuate is the southern part of peninsular Florida and the Florida Keys. If a storm approaching from east or west veers just a little toward the north as it nears landfall, your effort to escape could take you right into its path. If you live in any area where a scenario like this is possible, consider it especially important to get out early.

Evacuation Studies

Evacuation orders are not given lightly, so definitely take them seriously—very seriously. Refusal to go in extreme situations has many times in the past led to serious injury and death. Don't make your last words be, "over my dead body." Absolutely nothing, except perhaps the safety of a family member, is worth any unnecessary risk.

Evacuation studies have been ongoing for many years by federal and state agencies, often in conjunction with universities that have extensive meteorological curricula. They are designed to assist state and local governments in the development and enhancement of hurricane planning by providing the best technical information available.

These studies usually include related analyses that develop data concerning hurricane hazards, vulnerability of the population, assumptions about public response to evacuation advisories, evacuation network clearance times, and sheltering needs for various hurricane threat situations.

The results from these studies include analyses of storm surge situations, as well as evacuation requirements for hurricanes of different intensities and the various directions they come from (e.g., peninsular Florida is just as much at risk from hurricanes that approach from the west, out of the Gulf of Mexico, as from those coming ashore from the Atlantic).

Emergency planners use this and any other available pertinent information to compile checklists of steps to be taken before and during a hurricane. The overall objective is to provide emergency management officials with state-of-the-art information on the major factors affecting hurricane evacuation planning and decision making, and the skills and training aids necessary to educate the public.

It is important to note that storm surge maps reflect the worst-case scenarios of hurricane storm surge inundation (including astronomical high tide), regardless of the point where the center of the hurricane (or tropical storm) makes landfall. No single hurricane will necessarily cause all of the flooding represented on the maps. It should also be noted that these maps reflect only still-water saltwater flooding and do not take into account the effects of pounding waves that ride on top of the storm surge in locations exposed to wave action. In areas open to the coast these waves can be very large and can greatly exacerbate the damage already being caused by seawater flooding alone.

Also, storm surge maps do not show inland areas that may be flooded by excessive rainfall, which can take many forms. In a relatively flat area with small changes in elevation, flooding is often seemingly random, confined to deep ponding in those locations just a foot or two lower than their surroundings. Thus a few houses in one spot can be seriously inundated, while others just a block or two away remain high and dry.

Rainfall can also cause a sudden, sharp rise in lake levels, effectively flooding those houses nearby if the slope of the ground is low enough. Then there are rivers, which quickly reach flood stage and send acres of water to flood many square miles far beyond their banks.

Keep in mind that different storm surge zone categories suggest flooding is possible for your area for a storm of that category *or higher*. For example, a Category 3 storm surge zone would be most vulnerable to storms of Category 3 and higher, with a lesser risk for Category 2 or I. But, how can you actually be sure an oncoming storm will not be a Category 3 when it finally does come ashore?

Similarly, those people that live in Category 1 storm surge zones are vulnerable to all categories of storm, from 1 up to 5. Always remember that local officials will be making decisions about who should stay and who should go, so be sure to listen to and follow their advice if a storm is threatening your area.

Accuracy

Storm surge models are typically accurate about 80 percent of the time and for around 80 percent of the area they cover. Therefore, if the model calculates a peak 10-foot storm surge for an approaching hurricane, you can expect the actual peak to range from 8 to 12 feet. The model does account for astronomical tides (which can add significantly to the water height) because it specifies an average tide level. But, as mentioned earlier, these models also do not include rainfall amounts, river level increases, or wind-driven waves.

When it comes to determining flood zones, all of the information mentioned earlier is combined with the storm surge model to create the final analysis of at-risk areas. Obviously the precise point of the hurricane's landfall and its intensity at that time are crucial to determining which areas will actually be inundated by the storm surge. Where the hurricane forecast track or strength is inaccurate, the storm surge model will be correspondingly inaccurate. However, keep in mind that the flooding effect of rainfall will still apply.

Finding Shelter

Very often the best form of evacuation is simply to go to the nearest designated shelter, a hurricane-proof building in an area away from the risk of storm surge and other flooding. A designated American Red Cross shelter is always a good choice. Shelter locations will be broadcast frequently on radio and television, along with important information regarding how many they will hold, what you should bring with you, and whether or not pets are accepted. If you have pets and cannot take them with you, make plans for their well being in advance, too.

As a rule, most shelters will not take pets of any kind. So if you must leave them behind, put them in the most secure room in your house and leave at least a three-day supply of food and water. Also, make sure each pet has an identity tag or license with your address and telephone number on it.

All too often, shelter information is not broadcast until the situation becomes urgent. If you live in an evacuation zone, it would be a good idea to know well beforehand where you can go and what is involved in your staying there. A very good source for this information is your local office of the American Red Cross.

Know Before You Go

Finding a safe local shelter most often beats risking a long trip on the road, but if leaving the area is paramount, then plan carefully: not just your departure time, but also the route you will take. As a rule, your state's Department of Transportation determines which roads will serve as evacuation routes during emergencies. This information is typically available from the department's website in the form of maps, but don't wait until such information appears on television or in your local newspaper. By then it might be too late for an early start. Most states also offer this information on their Department of Transportation or Emergency Management Office website.

Equally important, if you plan to leave the area, know exactly where you plan to go. At least have a hotel or motel reservation far from the affected area, made in advance, if you do not have family members or friends to go to. A lot of other unhappy hurricane refugees will be looking too, and public shelters tend to fill rapidly. So if you have not made suitable arrangements in advance, you might well end up with nowhere to hide.

Returning Home

Areas that have been evacuated are prime targets for looters. As a result, many local law enforcement agencies post police officers, deputy sheriffs, or national guardsmen at access points to these communities. If you do not have definite proof, such as a driver's license or passport, that you live there, you will almost certainly be turned away. Keep this in mind when you leave home.

Also, if the area is deemed unsafe, regardless of proof of domicile, you can still be refused admittance. So have an alternate destination in mind, just in case.

CHAPTER 9
Protecting Your Property

There are two categories of property protection. First is the protection of your personal property: those important items that make up your life. Second, and certainly no less important since it also directly affects the protection of your personal property, is the protection of your home.

Personal Property

Some tough decisions are at times necessary here, so the first step is to prioritize. What are the most important items in the makeup of your life? Certainly among these should be such things as medications, especially prescription medicines. Always make sure you have at least a two-week supply of each medication on hand for everyone in your household because it could be a while before you will be able to reorder.

Protect critical documents from water damage with a waterproof box or heavy-duty plastic bag.

These might include copies of Social Security cards, passports, driver's licenses, birth certificates, wills, and other important instruments of personal identification. Financial documents should always be included: insurance papers on the house, car, and other expensive items; financial and tax records; deeds, titles, and mortgage records. It's also a good idea to have a contact list with addresses and telephone numbers that include doctors, banks, and other important institutions, agents who handle your insurance, utility companies, and family members who should be contacted in case of an emergency.

All these lists are, I know from personal experience, a lot of work to compile, but once you do it thoroughly for the first time, only minor updates are necessary to keep it current.

If you are computer-oriented and use one to keep your personal and financial records, or in a professional capacity, consider an external hard drive to maintain an up-to-date backup of all that information. Or buy a flash memory stick, sometimes known as a thumb drive. These have become very inexpensive in recent years, and have sufficient capacity to back up important documents that you might need to access immediately on a different computer, even if they don't have the capacity to store large numbers of high-resolution images. Unlike a hard drive that may not be as easy to access on a different computer (such as backing up a Macintosh and trying

An external hard drive for a computer, with a thumb-sized flash drive on top. *Photo by author.*

to read it with a PC), flash memory can instantly be read by any computer system that has a USB port.

If you use a Mac as your own computer and wish to able to read the files on a flash memory drive with a PC, first format the flash drive on a PC and then write the files to it with your Mac. If you are using a PC, all of your backup files can be read with a Mac without any additional formatting. This includes both an external hard drive and flash memory.

As for an external hard drive, that is still the best way to maintain long-term backups of data and image files too large for a thumb drive. And they too have become much cheaper in recent years. So, even if you lose your entire computer and related peripherals through flooding, as long as the hard drive was stored in a safe, dry place you will be able to quickly and easily rebuild all of your information.

Finally, there are those physical items representing a personal part of your life, such as photographs and mementos. You'll likely have far too much to save all of it, so just pick those most important first and then protect as much of the rest as time and space permit.

Your House

The best way to storm-proof your house is to use reliable code-approved coverings for *all* openings, especially those openings that have glass in them, such as windows and doors with glass insets. The importance of this cannot be stressed too much, because if the storm winds should get *inside* your house via a busted window or door, the chance of completely losing your roof increases significantly. And even if the roof doesn't go, the damage caused by wind and rain will be disastrous.

Do not waste your time taping windows. Tape does absolutely nothing to improve the strength of the glass, and it will not prevent that glass from shattering. But it will leave you with a sticky mess that is very difficult to remove once the storm has passed. One of the major hazards in a hurricane is wind-borne flying debris, such as tree branches, boards, and pieces of roofing, and it takes a substantial barrier to keep these outside.

In terms of cost, the biggest bang for the buck is the overlapping shutter. They are code-approved and come in aluminum, galvanized steel, and more recently, clear high-impact plastic. Both aluminum and clear plastic shutters are lighter than steel and somewhat more expensive, but they also will not rust and that's a major consideration if you live on or very close to the coast where they are subject to salt air. All of these shutters must be pre-installed by someone who knows how to do it correctly. The best installations include heavy-duty angle-aluminum tracks that are permanently mounted on both sides or the top and bottom of the opening. These tracks have threaded studs that allow each panel

These aluminum panels provide protection for a glass enclosed patio from the hurricane's winds. *Photo by author.*

to be mounted in seconds using wing nuts. The panels can be stored wherever convenient. Because of their light weight, they are easily handled by almost any adult or large child. Just don't wait until the wind is blowing too hard to try to carry them around.

Plywood is a little cheaper than metal shutters, but to be really safe you need at least 1/2-inch (many experts recommend 5/8- to 3/4-inch, especially for large windows). It works best if used in panels as large as possible, which makes them heavy and difficult to

These vertical tracks allow storm panels to be mounted horizontally. Note the top panel is mostly clear to allow light in.
Photo by author.

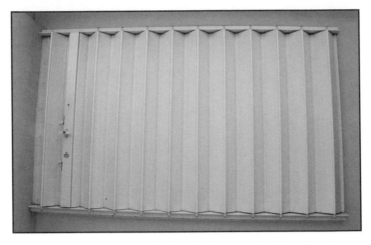

Accordion type hurricane window shutters can be closed and latched in just seconds. *Photo by author.*

handle, especially in any wind. Plywood also takes more time to install, and it suffers weather damage quickly in wind, rain, and sun. In the long term, metal panels are much cheaper and easier to store. Plywood takes up a lot more space in storage, and once wet it is often ruined.

The clear plastic panels are especially attractive to those who don't like that living-in-a-cave feeling that goes with metal or plywood shutters that block out all light. These panels are made of transparent, heavy-duty plastic that meets local codes and even passes the air cannon test. They are installed in the same manner as metal shutters, and cost a little more than the metal shutters. Some homeowners use just one of the clear shutters mixed in with metal shutters to get a comfortable level of light inside the house while at the same time reducing the overall cost of window shutters.

In terms of convenience, by far the most popular hurricane shutters today are the accordion style. Permanently mounted on either side of the opening, these heavy-duty aluminum shutters can be easily pulled together by hand in seconds to create a barrier

Accordion shutters in open position. *Photo by author.*

that meets the most stringent coastal county building codes. They are about three times more expensive than metal panels, but their convenience is a major asset. They also add significantly to the resale value of they house.

Another type of window protection that is gaining popularity, especially in the southern United States, is the aluminum Bahama shutter. It is hinged at the top, so that when the time comes it is simply lowered from its downward-angled position until it is flat with the side of the building, where it is secured with clips. These cost slightly more than accordion shutters, but they are also now available with small holes or louvers to allow some light into the room while at the same time keeping direct sunlight out, and this certainly does help keep air conditioning costs down. Thus in the long run there is a definite payback, and they also contribute greatly to the value of the house at resale because of their long-term durability.

Electric roll-down shutters are by far the most expensive. They also require regular maintenance to keep them working. And if you do opt for this very convenient form of protection, keep in mind that such shutters must also be equipped with a mechanical means of lowering and raising them if the power is off.

Another newer means of protection that is growing in popularity is shatterproof window glass. Just like the windshield on your automobile, this is a very strong

Hurricane-proof sturdy aluminum Bahama shutters can be lowered to completely cover the window. *Photo by author.*

clear plastic film sandwiched in between a double layer of permanently installed window glass. As of 2005, this glass was code-approved by Miami-Dade County, Florida, which has perhaps the toughest such standards in the country. Compared to normal window glass, it is several times more expensive. But also involved is the high cost of completely removing old windows and replacing them with these new designs, and for that reason shatterproof windows are for now mostly appearing in new construction.

High-impact window film, designed as a burglary deterrent, is also available. While it does not meet Miami-Dade windstorm codes, it does considerably improve the ability of the glass to withstand impact by flying debris. It must be permanently installed on existing glass by a qualified technician, and it does also reduce room heating (and fading of furnishings) by direct sunlight, so there is eventually significant payback.

A final note on shutters and panels: The rash of hurricanes in 2004 and 2005 brought out another type of scam artist—companies that collect hefty advances before starting installation, then never even start the work. Surprisingly, some of these have been local companies, both licensed and unlicensed. Not all of these probably started out to be scams; they simply got greedy and contracted for more work than they could do within the time specified. But the end result is still the same: Either way you don't have the shutters you paid for by the time the next hurricane season rolls around. So be careful and check out any company before you sign a contract and pay a big advance. And be very wary of any contractor from out of town.

The Roof

After windows and doors, your roof is likely the next weakest part of your house. Even if it only loses some shingles or tiles instead of the entire covering, the probability of damage skyrockets if any damage has previously occurred. Rain can enter through a partially compromised roof and flood the interior, resulting in widespread damage. Carpets and drapes are ruined; ceilings fall; walls are soaked; furniture, appliances, electronics, and clothing are a total loss. Just cleaning up the mess is expensive and a major effort, and that's before any repairs can even begin. Meanwhile mold and fungus begin to appear everywhere, creating a serious health hazard.

By far the most wind damage–resistant roof shape is the so-called hip design. The hip roof has no flat vertical surfaces at the ends, as does the very popular gabled roof. Thus every part of the roof has a slope, which allows the wind to flow over the top with far less resistance.

A flat roof also offers less wind resistance, but it has other vulnerabilities. In cold climates, heavy snow can pile up dangerously, and even in warm climates there is the problem created by standing water that eventually begins to seep through as the materials age. Pinhole leaks go unnoticed, often for years, until the underlying layers are seriously damaged and thus weakened, even though the surface layer still looks reasonably intact. The impact of flying debris in a situation like this can lead to the loss of most or all of the roof covering.

Your first step should be to make sure your existing roof is in good shape and also in compliance with local building codes in terms of materials and installation. This could even affect your insurance coverage.

The types of materials used to cover the roof decking vary considerably in cost and durability. The strongest roof is metal, now available in many shapes, finishes, and configurations that are far more attractive and up-to-date than the older flat-panel tin roof style. It is, unfortunately, the most expensive, but it will last far longer than any other material out there today, so in the long run it is probably among the least expensive.

There are many other different types of roofing materials available, from concrete shingle to barrel tile, on down to traditional asphalt shingles. The cheapest, and by far the least wind-resistant, are the so-called three-tab shingles. This is the most common shingle style used throughout the United States today. It is thin, soft, and easily lifted by a strong wind. It also has short life span. Given enough wind and time, it is easily torn completely off.

The next step up, and actually only slightly more expensive in terms of material cost, is the dimensional shingle. These shingles, when installed, have the irregular shape that looks much like a cedar shake roof. Each tile is far stiffer and more wind-resistant than the cheaper three-tab, and will last much longer.

One of the biggest costs in roofing is labor, which gets even more expensive with each passing year. And worst of all, trying to find a qualified roofing company to work on your house after a major storm has passed through your area is almost always beyond difficult. Many months will almost certainly pass before you can get any work done. And in the meantime your desperation makes you potential prey to unscrupulous fly-by-night roofers who do shoddy work that won't pass inspection and are likely not even licensed in your area.

There are two steps you can take beforehand to greatly reduce the potential for post-storm agony. First, if your roof is more than 10 years old, get it professionally inspected at least every other year. Annually is even better, especially for flat roofs. It may need repair work to survive a strong storm. If the roof has weak spots, all it may take is one strike by a piece of flying debris to cause enough damage for hurricane force winds to get a toehold. Once weakened roofing material starts to come up, the odds are the rest will go too, or at least enough of it to allow a serious amount of rainwater to get inside the house.

If it needs replacing, get a contract for the job right away. That way, even if a hurricane comes through and does serious damage to the roof before it can be replaced, you will at least be among the first in line for repairs or replacement as soon as the severe weather is over. Otherwise you will be forced to make endless telephone calls to all of the roofing companies in your

Blue and silver plastic tarps used to cover a hurricane-damaged roof. *Photo by author.*

area (who are also getting an endless number of calls from everyone else with a roof problem), and at best you will be at the end of a long line of others with the same problems. Expect a very long wait before help arrives, which could take up to a year or more.

If you live in an area that is particularly hurricane-prone, the logical second step is to buy and store a couple of large plastic tarps, big enough to cover roof damage immediately after the storm has passed. The blue plastic variety is light and compact for easier handling, and not expensive. And once installed it is good for up to a year before it deteriorates too much to provide protection. Trying to find tarps after a hurricane is difficult or even impossible, so get them before the season starts.

Installing these tarps as an emergency roof cover isn't difficult. On sloping roofs the tarp must be large enough to start two feet or so on the opposite side of the ridgeline and extend far enough down the slope to completely cover the damaged area. If the roof is flat, it must be large enough to cover the entire roof and hang down over the edges by a foot or so. Flat roofs are difficult to cover successfully, by the way.

If it is necessary to overlap two or more tarps to get sufficient coverage, make sure the overlap extends for several feet. This works pretty well on a sloped roof. The only way to overlap on a flat roof is by using a piece of lumber at least two inches thick underneath the area where both tarps overlap by at least two feet to create a tent effect. Sometimes this works well enough to significantly reduce water damage inside the house. It's worth a try and definitely better than nothing.

In order to keep these tarps in place, it is necessary to nail strips of wood along all exposed edges; otherwise, even a relatively low-velocity wind will eventually tear them loose or cause rips that leak. Remember, the tarps may have to stay up there for many months.

Ultimately, tarps are only an emergency measure and do not always work as well as we'd like. The only surefire protection is to keep the covering on your roof

Wind turbines like this one should be removed and the opening capped before the storm arrives. *Photo by author.*

in tip-top shape at all times, and in the long run that is also the most cost-effective way (by a huge margin) to stay protected.

Rooftop wind turbines are not nearly as popular today as they were 20 to 30 years ago, mostly because they have been demonstrated to have little effect on attic temperatures. But there are still plenty of them around and they do significantly increase the vulnerability of the roof to hurricane wind and water damage. There is always a high probability they will blow off during a strong storm, leaving a large gaping hole in the roof where water can pour in. If you have any wind turbines

A 2x8 is used as a brace to strengthen this double gate. *Photo by author.*

on your roof, completely remove them and cover the opening long before the hurricane is predicted to reach your area. Such coverings are available at the same building supply stores that sell turbines. Don't wait until the last minute to go looking for them; by then there may be none left in your area.

Fencing

Wooden fences are very vulnerable to hurricane-force winds. The stockade type (boards fitted tightly together) and the board-on-board variety have virtually no openings to allow the wind to pass through, making them the most susceptible to wind damage. One way

A suitable length of heavy-wall pipe is anchored to the gate at one end and the concrete pad at the other. This considerably increases the wind resistance of the gate. *Photo by author.*

to reduce the wind loading is to remove every other board and stack them where the wind cannot get to them, if you have time. Otherwise, at least try to brace any gates as much as possible. I have a large double gate in my fence, which I brace with a 12-foot 2x10 on the outside, plus a leaning brace on the inside made of heavy-wall 2-inch pipe that's anchored at the bottom on the concrete pad with a large lag bolt, and also at the top with another bolt. I lost part of my fence in Hurricane Wilma (2005), but the most expensive part—the gate—survived undamaged.

Trees

Each year a great many houses that would have otherwise survived a severe hurricane are severely damaged or destroyed by trees falling on them. Almost all of this is preventable by properly trimming those trees that are close enough to the house to cause damage. This should be done by a qualified arborist so that the canopy is properly thinned and shaped to reduce wind loading. They will look a lot better, too. I have mine done every other year in late winter or early spring, and I've convinced my neighbors to do the same, so that we all get a "bulk price" for the job.

If you have trees planted so close to the house that they can bend far enough make contact with the edge of the roof during hurricane-force winds, they should be removed completely or at least moved farther from the house. Constant banging against the edge of the roof will eventually loosen shingles or tiles, and once that starts, the wind gets a toehold and you stand a good chance of losing most, if not all, of its waterproof covering—a certain recipe for house flooding by heavy rains.

Trees planted too close to the edge of the roof can cause considerable damage in high winds even if they remain upright.
Photos by author.

Automobiles and Boats

Sometimes there are municipal parking garages available that offer automobile protection, but in many areas such spaces are hard to come by. Most of us will simply have to figure out which side of the house offers the best protection. I try to pick a spot that will most likely be on the downwind side of the house with as little chance as possible that a tree will fall on it.

If you do not have protected indoor storage for your trailered boat, treat it in the same fashion as your car. Just make sure the boat is tied securely to the trailer, and the trailer is anchored as securely as possible. If you don't have something substantial to tie it to, consider using a three- or four-point anchoring system with screw-into-the-ground anchors designed for house trailers. If you keep the boat on a concrete pad and feel the location is safe, add a four-point tiedown system near the edges of the pad using heavy-duty eyebolts secured to the concrete.

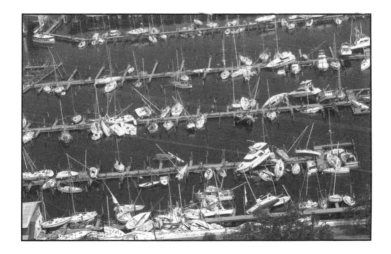

Damage to a marina near New Orleans by Hurricane Katrina in 2005. *FEMA photo by Win Henderson.*

Even the hurricane gods display a sense of humor now and then. This kayak was carefully deposited on the sign in Flamingo, Florida, by Hurricane Katrina in August 2005. *Photo by author.*

If you have a truly tight-fitting heavy-duty cover for your boat—one that you're sure the wind won't blow off—by all means keep the boat covered and wrap extra ropes over it as reinforcement. And also leave all drain plugs out so the boat won't fill up with water. The extra weight can do serious damage to the hull.

If you keep your boat at a marina and don't have time to move it to a hurricane-safe mooring inland somewhere, your only recourse will be to add extra lines to secure it to the dock. You will need enough extra mooring lines to double all of them, and chafing gear as well to protect those lines in places where they will rub against hard surfaces. Old garden hose or vinyl tubing will do just fine for this.

Attach all lines as high on pilings as practical to allow for extra-high tides and storm surge. Rig crossing spring lines fore and aft to keep the boat from being pushed into or up under the dock or the boat next to it. Adding fenders or old tires along the sides of your boat can help reduce impact damage. Fully charge all batteries to keep automatic bilge pumps running as long as possible. Don't leave any loose gear on deck, and seal all openings that could allow water to get into the interior. Duct tape (not masking tape!) around the edges of doors, hatches, and windows is a good idea.

During a recent hurricane in Miami, a friend of mine, having no safe place to leave his 25-footer, took it out into the shallows of Biscayne Bay and used two very heavy anchors with good holding power in the soft bottom to secure it. The anchors were placed one well ahead of the other with separate lines, each almost 200 feet long. He sealed the boat as tightly as possible, and after the storm it was still there—and still afloat—having survived winds in excess of 100 mph.

Make a Plan

Remember, you may have only 24 hours or less to get ready, so have a plan at least in outline form. That way you can complete preparations in an orderly, prioritized manner, and you'll be far less likely to overlook something critical or "discover" it at the last minute. Do what you can conveniently do at the very beginning of the hurricane season (June 1) so that you won't be frantically scrambling at the last minute as the big blow comes ashore.

CHAPTER 10
Windstorm and Flood Insurance

Until 1992, when Hurricane Andrew came ashore in south Florida and Louisiana causing damage that ultimately exceeded $31 billion, windstorm insurance for the average house in coastal states was relatively inexpensive. Andrew not only revealed that the companies who provided this coverage did not have cash reserves to cover those unexpected losses, it also uncovered a real cancer in the construction of many homes: shoddy materials and workmanship, which of course ultimately contributed significantly to the total damage cost, and in the aftermath, to skyrocketing windstorm insurance rates.

Just because you have homeowner's insurance does not mean you automatically also have windstorm (hurricane) coverage. You must specifically elect to include **windstorm coverage**, as well as **flood insurance**. Many unfortunates learned this lesson the hard way in New Orleans after Katrina in 2005.

Following Andrew, the insurance companies began raising their windstorm coverage rates substantially—doubling them in the first year alone. And they have continued to rise almost every year since then. If you are a homeowner with a mortgage, almost certainly your lender requires full insurance on your house, and that includes both windstorm and, if deemed necessary, flood insurance as well (which has also gone up significantly).

Windstorm insurance for the average house in Florida and other coastal states was around $400 before Andrew in 1992; by 2000 it had risen to $2,000 or more in some of these areas. Many homeowners who are not required by their mortgages to keep such coverage have since elected to drop it and bear the risk themselves. Others elected to keep the coverage, but to take the maximum deductible, at 15 percent with most insurance companies. Doing this means you are in effect self-insuring for the difference should you get damaged by a severe hurricane, so it would be prudent to set aside funds just for this purpose in some sort of interest-bearing account. If your house is insured for $400,000, for example, you could be looking at a deductible of up to $60,000.

Don't overlook the contents of the house when buying insurance. You should be able to document these items after the storm, as well as proof of ownership. Photographs are a good way to do this, as well

Damage south of Miami by Hurricane Andrew (Category 5, 1992).
FEMA photo by Bob Epstein.

as a bill of sale or professional appraisal for each of the more expensive objects. Make a detailed list of everything that has to be repaired or replaced.

Keep in mind that problems can arise when making a claim for unusual items like jewelry, artwork, furs, and antiques without receipts or documentation. It is really best that you have separate insurance riders for expensive items, and appraisals for unique or valuable items such as works of art. Receipts and appraisal documentation belong in your safe deposit box or another location where they cannot be lost during the storm.

Windstorm Insurance

Ever since Hurricane Andrew, a Category 5, so severely impacted southern Florida in 1992, the cost of windstorm insurance has risen rapidly. But, in an effort to make the cost more manageable for those homeowners who have spent a significant sum to "harden" their older homes against hurricane wind damage, insurance companies in many coastal states started a windstorm mitigation inspection program just before the 2012 hurricane season.

These inspections are mostly conducted by licensed building contractors and typically take about two hours. The inspector takes detailed color digital photographs of the areas considered most vulnerable to damage: doors, windows, roofs, and any other openings, for example. If all openings are protected by building code-approved covers, such as removable panels, or the doors and windows themselves have a code-approved hurricane rating, they are given a "passed" rating by the insurance company. Many new

Roof truss strap and plate: The strap goes across the top of the truss and is anchored on both sides to the concrete tie beam. The plate joins the ends of the truss together to make the entire assembly much stronger. *Photo by author.*

homes in hurricane-prone areas are also now being built with hurricane-rated doors, windows, etc.

The same rating considerations apply to the roof. If it has a code-approved covering (e.g. shingles, tiles, etc.) and the trusses are properly anchored to the tie beam with approved tie-downs, it too will be given a

A hip roof like this, with all sides sloping, is much more resistant to wind damage than a gabled roof. *Photo by author.*

"passed" rating. The type of roof (geometric shape) also figures into the premium. A hip roof is considered by its shape to be the most wind-resistant, for example. If the roof also has a secondary water-resistant layer, such as a Sealed Roof Deck, that too will help lower the premium.

If the inspection reveals that all areas passed, the homeowner gets the lowest available premium for his or her location. However, that rate also goes up for each opening or roof deficiency noted, so even one such deficiency will result in a significant rate increase.

Following the inspection the homeowner will receive a written report detailing the results. If any deficiencies are noted, it is up to the homeowner to get them corrected before the next hurricane season and to also furnish proof to the insurance company. If, however, you have one of these inspections of your house and feel there are errors in the report, by all means contact the company that performed the inspection and request your home be re-inspected.

After the Storm

If your house has suffered any damage, you should contact your insurance company as quickly as possible by any means at your disposal. Time is very important; the sooner you can get an adjuster to your house, the sooner the repair process can get started. You must have all of your insurance policy information on hand, including the policy number and the telephone number to call to file a claim. And by all means keep a detailed record of all communications with your insurance company, just in case there's a claims dispute later on. Save all paperwork you receive from your insurance company, its agent, or the adjuster.

It is also a good idea to take photographs of all the damaged areas. They could be invaluable in justifying a claim.

A gabled roof. The flat ends of this type roof are more prone to wind damage in a hurricane than a hip roof. *Photo by author.*

Keep in mind that while the windstorm coverage in a typical homeowner's policy certainly covers wind damage, it only covers water damage that is a direct result of rain entering through a wind-damaged area, such as a broken window or door, or a hole in the roof caused by flying debris, or roofing material that has been stripped off by the wind. It will *not* cover damage by flooding. You must have flood insurance to be protected for that. For more detailed information on your own flood risk and your cost of flood insurance, go to the website https://www.floodsmart.gov/floodsmart/.

You should familiarize yourself with all details of the coverage offered under your homeowner's policy. It may also cover resulting fire or vandalism, debris removal and repairs, and cash or replacement value of damaged property. There may be a provision for additional living expenses, should it become necessary for you to stay at a hotel if your home becomes unlivable. You may have to elect to have that provision added to your policy by calling your insurance company.

You want to get an insurance adjuster on site as quickly as possible. Keep in mind that insurance adjusters are specially trained to tell the difference between flood and hurricane damage. However, when a large number of claims are filed in any given area following a severe storm, the number of adjusters your insurance company has on hand may be spread thin and thus professional independent adjusters may be called in to help. Since the qualifications vary among insurance professionals, you might find yourself protesting the claim, if you think it has been wrongfully determined by an inexperienced adjuster. You can also file a complaint with your state insurance department, or as a last resort hire an attorney to continue the fight.

Damage to a car or boat should be reported to the company that provides your insurance for those items, not to your homeowner's insurance company.

But, what happens if you have a mortgage and your lender has failed to pay your homeowner's insurance (funds for this are usually included in your escrow account)? It's a rare situation, but it is an administrative oversight that has happened. However, under current law in a situation like this the mortgage company is now responsible for any damage to your property that would have been covered by your insurance. Also, all costs and fees to reinstate the insurance must be paid by the mortgage company if the insurer did indeed send notice of the payment due.

As for repairs, don't be rushed into signing a contract with just any roofing or building company. Make sure they are licensed to work in your area. If you feel you have enough time, collect business cards and get written estimates for the proposed job. Be especially wary of building contractors who encourage you to spend a lot of money on temporary repairs. If there is the slightest doubt in your mind, investigate the track record of any roofer, builder, or contractor that you consider hiring. Look for professionals and get references. You can also call the Better Business Bureau for help.

Never, and I cannot emphasize this enough, *never* give anyone a deposit until you have done your homework. Far too many unwary homeowners, desperate to get serious damage repaired after a severe hurricane, gave large down payments to unscrupulous contractors who soon disappeared after performing shoddy work, if indeed they performed any work at all. These thieves come out of the woodwork following any large-scale disaster.

Additional Recovery Steps

Safety first! Avoid loose or dangling power lines and report them immediately to the power company, police, or fire department. If you evacuated before the storm, when you return you should enter your home with caution. You might find snakes, biting insects, and wild animals looking for shelter from the storm and flooding.

Open windows and doors to ventilate and dry your home, if the weather allows. But at the same time be mindful that rainy, windy weather could come along at any time and cause further damage if it finds entry.

If you left any food in the refrigerator or freezer, check for spoilage. A tip for dealing with large amounts of spoiled food in your freezer: keep all meats and fish in the largest open-top plastic tubs that will fit in your freezer. That way if there is spoilage, you only have to remove and discard the tubs with their rotten contents and then leave the door open to air out the interior. I learned this the hard way many years ago, while spending several very unpleasant hours cleaning out a sickening mess instead of enjoying a Superbowl game on TV, just because my garage freezer decided to die suddenly.

Drive only if absolutely necessary! Avoid flooded roads and washed-out bridges that could be masking water that's deeper than you expect. Use your telephone only for emergency calls. If you have a cell phone, you should have charged it fully before the storm arrived. Use it sparingly until you get power back unless you have an emergency generator to power its charger.

Gas leaks are common following any severe hurricane that leaves a lot of structural damage in its wake. If you detect anything that smells like gas, or hear an unexplained hissing noise, immediately leave and call the gas company. *Do not* turn any lights or appliances on or off, since even the tiniest spark could trigger an explosion.

Just because your house lost electrical power during the storm does not mean it cannot come back on at any time with no advance warning, and the electrical company will not notify you before it suddenly turns the power back on. As soon as the power goes off, or before you evacuate, turn off the air conditioning system and any

Using large plastic containers like this to hold food inside a freezer makes cleaning easy. If the contents should spoil, just throw containers with contents still inside directly into the garbage can.
Photo by author.

other non-critical appliances, such a computers, televisions, etc. Do not turn off refrigerators or freezers, which should have been set for the lowest temperature 24 hours before the storm arrived anyway, unless you have a power fluctuation problem like that described in Chapter 12.

When the power finally comes back on, if you see sparks or broken or frayed wires, turn off the electricity at the main breaker. But if you have to step in water to get to the fuse box or circuit breaker, call an electrician first.

Use your nose to check for sewage seepage, and look carefully for water line damage. A dramatic loss in water pressure at the faucet might indicate a leak, although it might also simply be a water line pressure loss throughout your area. If you suspect any such damage in your house, avoid using the toilets and call a plumber. If water pipes are damaged, contact the water company and avoid drinking tap water, which should always be considered unsafe for human consumption until otherwise directed by the water company. If you have no way to boil water (don't waste precious camp stove fuel unless necessary), you can still use tap water by treating it with 15 drops of bleach per gallon as described in Chapter 14.

CHAPTER 11
Emergency Generators

Before rushing out to buy an emergency generator, there are a number of factors about its selection, maintenance, and use that must be carefully considered. First among these is how big (how many watts of output) should it be? Where will it be stored? Where will it be used? What type of fuel does it use and how should that be stored? How should it be connected to your house?

Choosing the Right Size

Because a hurricane is a tropical event, it is almost always (except in extreme northern latitudes) accompanied by warm, moist tropical air that lingers long after its passage—which often means hot, humid, and often rainy weather for days afterward. So naturally you would like to run your air conditioning system even after you have lost power from your local utility company. Just how practical is it to do this with an emergency generator?

In most cases, this is simply not very practical. Let's do the math: a 36,000 BTU central AC system—typical for the average three-bedroom, two-bath house—requires 4,500 to 6,500 watts to run the entire system, and almost three times that (12,000 to 18,000 watts, or 12 to 18 kW) just to get it started (this is called the startup load). So you must figure on at least a 12 to 15 kW generator just for the air conditioner alone. Add a refrigerator, and you're looking at an additional 2,000 to 3,500 watts (2 to 3.5 kW) to get it started. If you have an additional stand-alone freezer, figure yet another load similar to the refrigerator.

Of course, you want several electric lights (forget about using that power-hungry electric stove), and perhaps a fan or two. Add another 500 to 700 watts for those (assuming by now you have replaced all the incandescent lightbulbs in your house with CFLs—compact fluorescent lights—which use about a quarter of the watts needed for their incandescent equivalent). So now you're looking at a total startup load of around 12 to 15 kW for the air conditioner, plus another 2 to 3 kW for each refrigerator or freezer, and electric lights and fans for another 1 to 2 kW. To be safe, the generator must be able to handle the sum total of all startup loads at once, or you risk serious damage to most, if not all appliances: air conditioning and refrigerator or freezer compressors, and even the generator itself.

A typical 5 kW portable generator. The five gallons of gas in the can will run it for 10 hours. *Photo by author.*

So, to run a central air conditioning system and everything else in an average-size house safely, you'll need a 15 to 20 kW generator. It takes a fairly big gasoline engine to run a generator of that size, so you are looking at three to four gallons of gas per hour to keep it going. That can add up to almost 100 gallons of gasoline for a full 24-hour day. Where and how are you going to safely store it—especially enough to run the system for a full week? And where are you going to buy more in such large quantities if you run out before power is restored?

Remember, when the power is out over a large area, as always happens after a major hurricane, it may take weeks for full restoration. Until then, even when you do find an open gas station, you can also bet on long lines, many hours of waiting, and likely rationing.

However, most large-capacity generators (15,000 watts or larger) are usually powered by diesel, propane, or natural gas. For anything other than piped-in natural gas you must figure on a permanent tank big enough to store the amount of fuel needed to run it for at least one week—and even that might not be enough in a severe situation like Hurricane Katrina's massive damage along the Gulf of Mexico coast in 2005. For most generators of that size, the fuel of choice is propane or diesel. Natural gas, if piped in, is by far the most convenient but not as energy efficient, so you would likely have to choose a generator of around 20 kW to get 15 kW output. And, what will you do if the hurricane also disrupts the availability of natural gas in your area?

Standby generators of that capacity are also expensive, and require a permanent installation with local permits and a hurricane-proof shelter. The total cost for this typically runs $7,000 and up, and that doesn't even include a storage tank and the large quantity of fuel needed to run the system for at least a week.

Size Definitely Matters

I have a system that I've used for years, through three hurricanes, to survive in reasonable comfort without air conditioning. It requires a 4 to 5 kW gasoline generator for up to two typical refrigerators or freezers, plus lights, and one or two fans. For just one refrigerator/freezer plus lights and fans, figure 3 to 3.5 kW.

This system does not require 24 hours of non-stop generator operation; I've found I can get by in reasonable comfort using it for just five to six hours per day: Two hours in the morning just after sunrise, one to two more around noon, and another two in the evening around dinner time. During those periods I also use the generator to run a couple of fans, a few lights, and a 12-volt battery charger. With a load like this, my 5,200-watt generator burns just under a half-gallon per hour, or two to three gallons per day.

Such small quantities of gasoline are a lot easier to buy and transport, and are much safer to store for a short time, at least long enough to get through the hurricane season, after which any that's unused goes into the family auto.

With this system I'm able to keep my refrigerator and freezer cold enough to get by on a day-to-day basis. I'm also able to charge several small automotive batteries that I use to power my small 12-volt (automotive-type) fans. Just one of these per bedroom makes all the difference in overnight comfort, and one battery will usually keep one fan running for up to two or three nights between charges. Gasoline generators of this type range in price from $500 to $1,200, depending upon whether they're hand-cranked or electric start.

Therefore, in the long run it makes sense never to buy more generator than you really need. Bigger generators burn more fuel. A 5 or 6 kW generator runs for around two hours on a gallon of fuel, while a 3.5kW model will go for up to three hours on the same amount.

Storage and Safe Operation

Most likely you'll store a small generator in the garage, so get one with wheels; it will be a lot easier to move.

Never, and I mean *never* in the strongest possible words, run a generator anywhere in the house or garage, even with all doors and windows open. Don't run it outside the house near an open window, either. Carbon monoxide (CO) is completely odorless and can build up quickly, with fatal consequences. Every year there are far too many fatalities (and lots of very close calls as well) from CO produced by emergency generators in use during power outages. Don't take *any* chances!

Always run the generator outside, under some sort of cover that will protect it from rain. And keep all windows tightly shut on that side of the house while it is

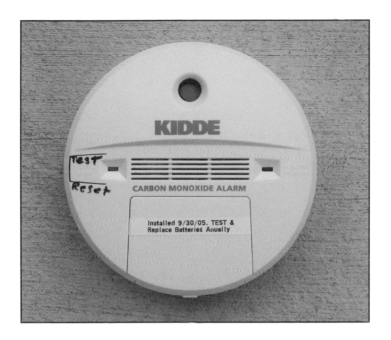

A carbon monoxide alarm. Every house using a portable generator anywhere on the premises or a propane camp stove inside should have one of these, plus smoke alarms as well. *Photo by author.*

running—and for at least 30 minutes after shutting it off—to keep the CO where it belongs: outside. Most likely you will want to do this anyway because of the annoying racket most of these generators make.

And just to be extra safe, buy at least one battery-operated carbon monoxide detector/alarm ($20 to $25). It could save your life.

A tip: always keep and use the generator in a secure location (at least chain it to something solid). Theft is inevitably a major problem during every post-hurricane crisis.

Connecting the Generator to House Wiring

If you want to connect your generator to the house wiring, you must first have a qualified electrician install a code-approved switch that completely disconnects your house from the utility company's power grid. Otherwise you'll also be trying to power everyone in your neighborhood, and the generator won't handle that. Plus, anyone who touches any of the wiring anywhere along that part of the grid is in danger of electrocution. You certainly don't want to injure or kill a neighbor or perhaps the very person who is working so hard to restore the power to your house.

Don't try to get by with pulling the master fuse in your fuse box. This will not completely disconnect your house from the power grid. The National Electric Code *requires* the use of an approved power shutoff switch, which when installed by a qualified electrician will typically cost from $400 to $600, including the wiring between the generator and the house.

Otherwise, your best bet is to connect heavy-duty extension cords directly from the generator to the various loads it will be running. And just to avoid any risk of overloading the generator, connect them to heavy loads such as a refrigerator or freezer one at a time so that the generator doesn't have to deal with the startup load of all of them at the same time.

Generator Maintenance

I treat the gasoline in the tank of my generator with a fuel stabilizer, such as PRI-G (Power Research Inc., *www.priproducts.com, 888-776-937*) as well as any other gasoline stored in cans, as soon as I buy it. Fuel stabilizers keep the gasoline from breaking down with age for at least two years, a process that otherwise will start in just a few months. Left untreated, in less than a year gasoline eventually becomes a gummy mess that doesn't even smell like gasoline. This process happens even faster in a warm, humid climate; the results will gum up the tank and carburetor to the point that the generator will not start and an expensive cleanout is required.

Every month or so I start my generator and run it for 10 to 15 minutes with a small load on it, such as an electric light, just to make sure it is still capable of outputting AC power. At the end of the session I turn off the gas at the tank so that all of the fuel left in the carburetor is completely burned by the time the generator shuts down on its own. Fuel left in the carburetor will

Using a fuel stabilizer like this will extend the usable life of gasoline by several years. *Photo by author.*

otherwise evaporate over time and clog the jets, which means expensive repairs.

By all means change the oil according to the owner's manual, but never less than once per year. A good time to do this is just before the beginning of the coming hurricane season.

With proper use and maintenance a generator will last for many, many years. I know of some that are over 20 years old and still running just fine, including the one I replaced just 2 years ago.

Solar Power

The technology for generating electrical power with sunlight has been around for many years, but more recently it has begun to show promise that really appeals to the homeowner. It is conceivable that this system could, at some point, eliminate all need for emergency generators powered by gasoline, diesel, propane, or natural gas. The advantages of this system are many: no noise, no dangerous exhaust fumes, no need to store fuel, and no maintenance.

A solar system uses rooftop panels that convert sunlight into DC electrical power. An inverter converts this DC into the AC needed to run our lighting and appliances. Unless there is a need to store electrical energy on site, any AC electricity not needed to run your house at any given time is "sold" to your local power company by feeding it right into that company's electrical grid. In effect, the meter on your house runs backward at the time, thereby reducing your electric bill.

Even when your solar system is not generating all of the power you need at the moment, your electric meter still runs more slowly, thereby reducing your electric bill.

In other words, if your solar system generates half of the electricity your house needs, then your bill is also reduced by half. If your system generates 80 percent of your power needs, then your bill will be only 20 percent of what it otherwise would have been.

As this is being written, solar power installations are still somewhat expensive; nevertheless even at this time a system capable of supplying 80 percent of your electrical need should pay for itself in about eight to nine years. And there are also federal tax credits, sometimes as well as subsidies, that help reduce the cost of installation.

No surprise, then, that more and more homes are adding solar power. Over the last seven or eight years almost 40,000 homes have gone that route. And as the expense of installation continues to decrease, while the cost of electricity supplied by your power company is expected to continue to increase, the economics of solar power should steadily become ever more appealing.

By the way, the latest rooftop solar panels are a far cry from the old bulky systems that had to be bolted down on top of the roof and often created leak problems, as well as offering a wind-resistant high profile that could cause their loss or damage in a hurricane. The new generation is about as thick as a rubber doormat, and an adhesive is used to hold them in place.

One note, however: if you want electricity at night when there is no power available from your electric company, as would possibly be the case after a hurricane, then you will also need enough batteries of sufficient capacity on hand to provide power after dark. As a minimum, the solar system you would want to install should be able to at least deliver enough power to keep all critical appliances going: refrigerator, freezer, enough lights, and fans. In other words, just what an emergency generator would have covered.

For more information on solar power incentives that are available for your part of the country, go to the website http://dsireusa.org, which is the Database of State Incentives for Renewables and Efficiency.

CHAPTER 12
Losing Power

Losing power during or immediately after a hurricane is likely, and if the storm is stronger than a weak Category 1, it's a given. If this doesn't happen to you, just say a little prayer and thank your lucky stars, but still expect that it will happen when the next storm comes marching in. It could even happen after the storm has passed because of problems elsewhere on the grid. Expecting the worst and being ready to deal with it is a necessary (but brief) part of pre-storm preparation.

Sometimes, when the power goes, it just shuts off like flipping a light switch. This does no harm to your appliances, any more than when you pull the plug or the power just goes off unexpectedly. But once it does go, because of the nature of hurricanes, there are several important steps you should take right away.

Turn off all air conditioning. Also, turn off all other appliances that are especially sensitive to power surges, such as computers, televisions, audio equipment, and so on. Make sure they are completely off, not just on standby. If in doubt, pull the plug.

Refrigerators and freezers are pretty tough and are generally built to deal with momentary power surges, and besides, you don't want to turn them off and then forget they are still off when the power does come back on. But if the power is fluctuating wildly, all those repeated suddenly on, suddenly off cycles will eventually do some damage. In situations like this it is a good idea to pull the plug, and then tape a note on the door stating that this has been done.

By far, even worse than simply losing power is when it repeatedly and rapidly cycles on and off, or goes into a low-voltage "brownout" mode. This is a situation often encountered in areas not yet directly affected by the strongest winds of the hurricane. It happens primarily because the location where the storm is actually doing most of its dirty work is suffering an ongoing series of local power failures which spread outwards along the grid like ripples in a pond, and ultimately affect a much larger area. This can cause your electrical power to alternate between voltage surges, brownouts, and momentary blackouts. This situation is tough on everything, so your best bet is to shut down all appliances—even refrigerators and freezers as mentioned above—until this destructive cycle stops.

After the storm is over, it is not uncommon for power to come back on for a few seconds or minutes, then go off again, and possibly repeat this several times, or for the voltage to wildly surge up and down before reaching stability. That's why it is a good idea to wait at least 30 minutes after the last interruption to turn everything back on. Once you are satisfied that the power is on and stable, then you can begin to restart the air conditioning, and turn refrigerators and freezers on again.

Electrical power is lost during a hurricane for a variety of reasons. One of the most common is overhead transmission lines being broken by flailing tree branches in high winds, flying debris, and falling trees. Tree branches are the single largest cause. This type of damage could be significantly reduced with better and more frequent trimming around power lines. But the power company is always sandwiched between a public that wants cheaper electricity and a need to be profitable enough to stay in business. Tree trimming is an expensive form of manual labor that also takes a lot of time. And it never stops.

And believe it or not, many homeowners also loudly raise hell when the power company shows up to trim trees that crowd power lines in their yards. As a result, many trees that need serious trimming do not get cut sufficiently, if at all, and thus many of us have to suffer through unnecessary power loss due to the intransigence of a few. Some municipalities have recently recognized this and subsequently passed ordinances that allow power companies to trim where necessary.

Unfortunately, knocking down one transmission line doesn't affect just one house. Often everyone in the immediate neighborhood loses power, too. Sometimes this triggers a domino effect, and other parts of the power grid shut down as well, causing failure for even more homes.

Also, when thousands of such lines are taken out, each one must be repaired—one at a time. Extra repair crews may be brought in from other states as necessary. The work continues day and night, but it can still take weeks before your area gets its power back, because the power company prioritizes these repairs according to the number of customers affected by each one. If your outage affects only a few houses in your neighborhood, you could be one of the last to get electricity back.

If the power outage is really widespread, it may take a month of more for the restoration process to be 100 percent complete. However, much to my surprise, after Hurricane Wilma (October 2005) knocked out power to over 3.4 million customers throughout the southern third of the Florida peninsula, with lots help from power companies in neighboring states, all but some 5,400 customers had their electricity restored with three weeks. A good part of the reason for this speedy recovery is that Florida has had plenty of practice over the last few years, and a lot of valuable lessons were learned throughout the busy 2004 hurricane season.

Other causes of electrical power failure include grid overload, flooding of buried power lines, physical damage to substations by the storm, and so on. Underground power lines are obviously far less prone to breakage by trees and flying debris. The only problem with this solution is that removing existing overhead transmission lines and replacing them with underground cables is very expensive. Many power companies argue that this is not cost-effective. Unquestionably this is true for at least the short term, and whether or not it would also be valid long-term depends on how many severe storms strike that particular area in the years to come.

A less expensive alternative is to "harden" the existing overhead system by replacing poles that are too weak to withstand a strong wind, as well as a hard-nosed approach to keeping all trees that could strike transmission lines trimmed back sufficiently. But even these tactics are not cheap. And the poles needed to withstand hurricane force winds are often bigger and more unsightly, which almost no neighborhood is willing to accept without complaint.

Unfortunately, it is a human characteristic to eventually consign bad memories to those darkest recesses of our minds. And each year that goes by without a significant storm event tends to push those memories of the last severe hurricane further and further back. It typically takes less than a decade for most of us to forget what the fuss was all about. Add to this the growing ranks of newcomers who have never had to deal with a serious hurricane event and often do not have the foggiest notion of the threat they represent, and it does not take long for tree branches to enfold power lines, or for building codes to become a little weaker.

CHAPTER 13
Self-Preservation

Once the arriving hurricane begins to increase in intensity, your first thoughts must be directed toward the preservation of yourself, your family, and everyone else in your house at that time. Always keep some sort of general plan in mind to deal with the problems that are certain to arise.

By now all preparations should have long been completed, and you are settled in for whatever amount of time it takes to see this unwelcome event through. Typically it takes anywhere from 6 to more than 12 hours for the worst of the storm to pass, but in rare instances that period could be much longer. I was once stuck in a Category 3 hurricane in the Bahamas (Betsy, 1965) that seemed to go on forever. We were subjected to hurricane force winds for more than 24 straight hours. It was real test of patience and nerves, but we got through it by remaining inside a safe shelter until it was past.

If your house is protected by good storm shutters that cover all vulnerable openings—especially those with glass—and your roof is strong and in good condition, you may be looking forward to just staying put until the storm passes. But if things really start to go wrong, what should you do next?

A Safe Room

The best place to ride out the storm is in the safest room in your house. This is preferably a room with no windows, or if there are any windows they should be the smallest in the house, and adequately protected by storm shutters or heavy plywood. This would include most bathrooms, or better yet, a big closet, if there's enough room. You should already have that choice in mind long before the house starts to come apart. Even a shuttered window can fail if a big tree hits it, and injury from shattered glass becomes a real threat to your safety. The larger the window, obviously, the greater the threat (as it's a bigger target for airborne debris).

If you live in an area vulnerable to flooding or storm surge, stay away from any belowground shelters. Usually the first floor is your best bet—unless it begins to flood—because that is typically the strongest part of your house. And if there is any potential for flooding, and if your only escape route in that situation is through the roof, you should have an axe or strong pry bar on hand to force an opening through it should you become trapped in the attic by rising water.

I can certainly tell you from personal experience that it is indeed difficult to keep your cool when it sounds like the whole world is coming apart around you, when the wind is rising to a screaming pitch that is painful to the ears, and when outside your house you hear all sorts of scary crashing and banging noises. Each gust of wind sounds (and feels) like a giant fist slamming into the side of your house. But staying calm is exactly what you must do in a situation like this.

This is why you should already have a room of final refuge in mind long before it becomes necessary to go there. You should also have other necessities on hand, such as blankets for added protection. Many survivors have made it through severe storms—even tornadoes—by getting into the bathtub or the back of a closet and using a mattress for extra cover while their house came crashing down all around them.

Knowing just how safe your house really is— whether or not it is potentially strong enough to resist a severe hurricane—is another good reason for having it inspected by a wind certification service as outlined in Chapter 9. If there are any questions in your mind about its ability to survive such storms, your safest course of action is to evacuate well in advance.

If you want information about how to build a safe room and an estimate of the cost, download the PDF file "Building a Safe Room" from the following website: *www.nhc.noaa.gov/HAW2/pdf/building_safe_room.pdf.*

Keeping in touch via a 12-volt portable TV, cellphone, and weather radio. *Photo by author.*

Monitoring the Storm's Progress

If the hurricane is strong enough and close enough, it goes without saying that power will likely long since have failed. At this point you are understandably wondering when this will end. A battery-powered AM/FM radio is my first choice because there is almost always a station within reach that is still on the air. A NOAA weather radio is helpful, and not expensive, so I suggest you have one of those as well. But the nearest NOAA station in your area can also be knocked off the air, and then the weather radio isn't any help. That's why I prefer a broadcast radio as my first choice.

A battery-powered black-and-white TV is also not expensive. I've had one since just before Andrew in 1992; it was a terrific help back then and has been a good source of information during power failures through every other hurricane in my area since. But, as of recently, my old black-and-white TV will be useless because the entire broadcast television system is switching from analog to digital. So if you decide to buy a new battery-powered TV, make sure it is digital-ready. And a converter box for your old analog TV, unless it, too, is battery-powered, isn't a usable option in this situation.

It goes without saying that you should not even think about leaving the house while the hurricane is raging outside, unless of course it becomes an absolute emergency and you have no other option. Many unfortunates have been seriously injured and even killed by large pieces of flying debris. Keep some sort of plan for an emergency evacuation in mind, just in case. And keeping up with evacuation orders is a big reason to have a battery-powered radio or TV.

Don't be suckered into going outside by the near-calm conditions of the eye, should it come your way—another reason for keeping in touch. If the hurricane's eye actually does reach your area, the usual pattern is extreme wind followed very quickly by near

Damage south of Miami by Hurricane Andrew (Category 5, 1992). *FEMA photo by Bob Epstein.*

calm; there is seldom a long-term gradual decrease in velocity as would be the typical case when the storm is actually heading away from you. If at all possible, wait at least 30 minutes; an hour is even better because an extremely large, slow-moving hurricane may have a large eye that could take as much as an hour to pass.

And once it would seem that the storm has really passed, you want to be wary of sudden strong rain bands that might still come your way. These can produce high-velocity winds that may gust to hurricane force. Occasionally some of these rain bands may even contain a tornado, possibly hidden by heavy rain so that you never see it coming (although you might get some warning from its freight-train roaring sound—but don't count on it). So be safe, and stay indoors until notified by authorities that it is safe to travel in your area. Or, lacking that information, wait at least an additional hour or two after you first think it is probably safe to go out.

Myths and Reality

Considering the large number of hurricane landfalls in the United States during the first five years of the twenty-first century, you would think by now most folks would have become wise in the ways of these extremely dangerous tropical monsters. But unfortunately, that is not the case. To be sure, those of us who have experienced one or two of these events firsthand understand the reality. But many who live along the coast and who have thus far been spared, as well as the thousands of newcomers who move to coastal areas from well inland every year, still cling to myths and misconceptions that in reality could put them very much in harm's way.

Having spent my entire life living in hurricane-prone areas of the United States, I should think by now I've heard every hurricane myth there is; but each year someone seems to invent yet another "fact" that defies all logic.

It is an established fact that mobile homes are by far the most vulnerable structures in high-wind situations. Florida, the Gulf Coast, and many parts of the southeastern United States have thousands of mobile home communities. When it comes to evacuation, everyone who lives in a mobile home in a threatened area should not have to think twice about leaving. Yet thousands refuse to go every time, offering more silly excuses than a dog has fleas.

One justification that is heard all too frequently: "My mobile home is tied and braced, so it's safe to stay." Others include, "Hurricanes don't come this way anymore," and, "My mobile home has survived the high winds of many thunderstorms without damage, so it should be able to handle a hurricane."

The reality is that no matter how well a mobile home is tied down and braced, its overall construction is simply too flimsy to handle sustained high winds over a period of hours, even though with luck it may have managed to remain undamaged through a few brief strong thunderstorm wind gusts in years past. However, winds in excess of 100 mph are rare in even a severe thunderstorm, while a Category 4 or 5 hurricane can produce gusts that approach or possibly exceed 200 mph. Thunderstorm winds are almost always too brief to move large, heavy objects through the air, a common hazard in a hurricane. The walls and roof of a trailer or other lightly constructed building are simply too thin to offer any protection from this hazard.

Even living in a condo on the second floor or higher does not mean you are safe from the storm's winds and high water. Unless the building is solidly built to a code that offers real hurricane protection (many are not), it is no safer than a poorly constructed single-family home. And if there is not adequate protection for all windows (not just those facing the coast), they can fail too. As already mentioned in Chapter 5, the velocity of the wind increases with height. And even if the building escapes direct damage by storm surge or flooding, you could be trapped for days afterward without power or running water.

Even the tallest buildings have suffered severe window damage during strong hurricanes. If even one window is shattered, the falling glass becomes a swarm of sharp-edged missiles that take out other nearby unprotected windows.

It is not uncommon for long stretches of coastline to get by for years—even a decade or two in some instances—without being hit by a hurricane. But sooner or later the law of averages catches up, as in central Florida, which was struck by five major hurricanes in just two years (2004 and 2005) after experiencing only weak Category 1 storms for the previous 12 years.

Even many seasoned coastal residents still cling to the false belief that hurricanes only come during the official hurricane season (June 1 through November 30). Over the years, however, hurricanes and tropical storms have occurred somewhere in the Atlantic basin during every month of the year. The so-called hurricane season only means the highest probability of a U.S. hurricane landfall will take place sometime during the months of June through November, but don't dismiss the rest of the year. Thus far landfalls in the United States by these off-season storms have been rare, but it would be foolish to assume it can never happen.

A surprising number of homeowners apparently still feel that preparing their house with storm shutters and a well-maintained roof is a waste of time and money, "because a big hurricane will destroy it anyway, and that's what I have insurance for." The reality is that statistics show otherwise; most properly built and well-protected houses do get through a major hurricane with little or no damage. The odds strongly favor adequate preparation, which in the long run is still much, much cheaper than major repairs or rebuilding.

A destroyed or extensively damaged house docs not only mean the building will have to be rebuilt. It also means that the contents have been destroyed or severely damaged. And the probability of injury or death to anyone—even a cherished pet or two—inside at the time is much more likely. Then there is the agonizingly endless chore of getting the house rebuilt when contractors and building supplies are scarce as hens' teeth

The only house that survived here did so because of stronger construction. Gulf coast of Mississippi, Katrina, 2005.
FEMA photo by Mark Wolfe.

because of widespread damage in the area. The process will take many months in the best of circumstances, and often well over a year.

And just because you don't live on or near the coast does not mean you are immune to hurricane damage. You may be far enough inland to be free of any storm surge risk, but rain-induced large-area flooding and wind damage can reach well over 100 miles inland. You should be aware of the risks for your area and take the necessary precautions.

Finally, don't assume that the government will be there to take care of all your needs immediately after the storm has passed. Most likely it will take them at least one to three days to reach you after a major hurricane, and very likely their available resources at that time will be limited. You are by far your best and most dependable resource. But only if you did what you should have done and were properly prepared.

CHAPTER 14
Water and Food

Once the storm has passed, you should be settling into a routine that will make life as comfortable as possible until the power goes back on, the tap water is once again safe to drink, gasoline is readily available, and traffic on the roads is no longer a nightmare (at least no more of a nightmare than usual). If you followed the checklist in Chapter 7, you certainly won't have any reason to be out in hot, rainy weather immediately after the hurricane passes, standing in a long line perhaps to get a few jugs of water and maybe a sack or two of ice.

If you lack an emergency generator to power your refrigerator or freezer, obtaining more ice will sooner or later become your most immediate need. But that should be at least two to three days away if you use what you should have acquired before the storm sparingly. And if you did set your refrigerator to its lowest temperatures well before the storm, as already suggested, it will keep its contents cold for at least 24 hours so long as you open it as little and as briefly as possible. Ditto the freezer, which can go almost 72 hours before the food in it begins to reach outside temperature, especially if you filled all available space inside it with jugs of drinkable water and they had sufficient time to freeze solid before the power failed.

Water

It takes a lot of water to stay comfortable and healthy—on average a gallon per person per day just for drinking—so don't waste any that's potable. The water you should have stored in the bathtub and several plastic trashcans isn't for drinking, but rather for bathing, and also flushing the toilet if tap water fails.

If your supply of potable water begins to run low and you have a source of water that's questionable, such as tap water that is possibly contaminated because of pressure loss in the system, here is how that water can be made safely drinkable.

First, if there is any particulate in the water, filter it through a clean piece of fine-mesh cloth. If you have a way to boil it, do so for at least two to three minutes, then let it cool to room temperature. Once cool you can add 8 to 10 drops of laundry bleach per gallon and let stand for an additional 20 minutes before drinking. But if you don't have natural gas or electric power for the kitchen stove, don't use a camp stove for this purpose because it takes far too long and uses way too much fuel.

Storing empty plastic jugs that will be used to hold drinking water in a hurricane situation. *Photo by author.*

Instead of boiling, as long as the water appears clear, add 15 or 16 drops (16 drops = 1/2 teaspoon) of laundry bleach (such as Clorox) per gallon and shake well. Let stand for 20 minutes before drinking to ensure all bacteria are dead. By now the water should have a very slight odor of chlorine. If it doesn't, add another five or six drops, shake well, and let stand for 20 minutes. If it still does not smell faintly of chlorine, dump it and use water from another source.

That small amount of bleach will not harm you, and in fact I find I cannot even taste it. In any event, just be sure the water you are drinking is safe because a situation like this is unquestionably the worst possible time to get sick.

Toilets use a lot of water each time they are flushed — four to five gallons for the older style, two to three gallons for newer models. If tap water isn't available, try not to flush any more than absolutely necessary (that is, only for solid waste). If you find the odor offensive, add a few drops of a scented detergent like Pine Sol.

Showers are okay as long as you have running water. And if you also happen to have a gas hot water heater with gas still available, you are really in luck! Otherwise you will have to put up with stingy sponge baths, and then only when necessary.

Food

Eat the most perishable items first, or store them in a cooler with ice. Frozen items in the freezer will last longer than those in the refrigerator, so use up the unfrozen foods first before hitting the cooler or the freezer. Save the canned items as long as possible, but a word of

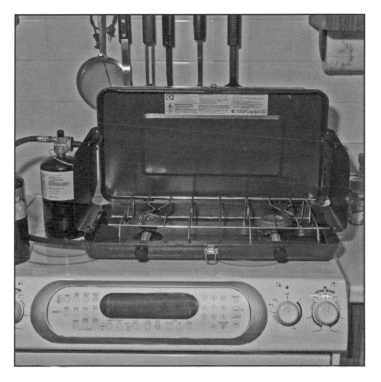

A two-burner portable propane camp stove with an extra one-pound cylinder of fuel. *Photo by author.*

caution here: do not open any cans that show signs of swelling, which could indicate dangerous bacteria inside. And any canned food past the "best if used by" date should get a thorough sniff test before being eaten. If any food is questionable for any reason, toss it.

You won't be able to use the kitchen stove if it is electric, until the power comes back on or unless you have a very big generator (see Chapter 11) because it consumes a lot of power. Most likely you'll have to use a gas grill, or a small propane camp stove. A basic two-burner camp stove is not expensive, nor are the small one-pound portable cylinders. If used as sparingly as possible, one of these small cylinders will last for at least a full day when cooking for two to three adults.

As an alternative, you can also buy propane in a 25-pound tank, but you will need a special hose fitting to connect it to most portable camp stoves. I prefer the small one-pound cylinders because they are easier to store, and they also make it easier to monitor how much fuel you are using and thus how much you have left. Propane is somewhat cheaper in a larger tank, but unless you use the stove a lot on a regular basis, the difference is not significant.

All propane stoves should be used in a well-ventilated area, because there is always a slight risk of carbon monoxide (CO) poisoning. To monitor CO accumulation from the cook stove, and from any generator you may have running outside, it is a good idea to have a carbon monoxide detector/alarm in the same room. Just be careful that you use the camp stove in a location where it is not a fire hazard. I find the top of my electric kitchen range is a good place for it, and my carbon monoxide detector is mounted on the wall just a few feet away.

While you are at it, if you don't have a couple of smoke alarms already located in strategic spots around the house, pick them up when you buy the carbon monoxide detector. And don't forget to change the batteries in all of them at least once a year. Make that a New Year's Day project, or the first day of each hurricane season, and you won't likely forget.

CHAPTER 15
Assessing the Damage

One of your first steps after the storm has safely passed will be to assess damage. If it is still dark and you cannot wait for daylight, use flashlights—not matches, candles, or anything else with an open flame, as there could be gas leaks. Even if you don't have gas at your house, what about your neighbors? Why survive a hurricane only to burn your house down afterward? It happens. You should also immediately clean up any spilled medicines, drugs, and other potentially harmful materials, especially if you have small children or pets.

Outside everything is wet, and there is almost certainly scattered debris and standing water. Avoid going out in the dark if at all possible, but if you must go, do so as safely and as briefly as you can. And even when daylight comes, definitely *do not* let your children play in any standing water. At the very least it could be contaminated with sewage, or worse—hiding a downed power line, sharp objects, or a dangerous open hole in the ground.

Interior damage caused by loss of roof covering during a hurricane.
Photo by author.

Stay away from damaged trees that could be unstable and come down at any time. Watch for debris underfoot that could contain nails and other sharp objects. Roofing materials almost always have rusty nails embedded, and also there is usually broken glass. Don't go barefoot, nor allow your children to do so.

Be ready at all times for an unexpected return of electric power. This can happen right after the storm passes in a few lucky neighborhoods, so don't get caught in a dangerous situation by its sudden and unanticipated reappearance.

Keep Off the Road

Unless you have an absolutely compelling reason to go out in your auto, don't. Traffic lights are down or out, many street and traffic signs have been blown into other zip codes, and debris is everywhere and often blocking the road. The accident rate skyrockets, tempers flare, and otherwise rational folks do stupid things. Save the gas in your tank for later, when you really need it.

Hurricane Andrew in 1992 had barely passed through Miami before cars filled with camera-toting rubberneckers arrived from unaffected parts of the county to cruise the streets of my neighborhood even as we were struggling to clear big trees and branches from the road in front of my house. Wherever the street was blocked by debris, these idiots simply drove right across lawns (including my own) which had been made soft by heavy rainfall, tearing up the grass and leaving deep, muddy ruts. As I've mentioned before, otherwise rational folks often do stupid, thoughtless things in such situations.

You should expect to encounter lots of roofing materials, pieces of glass, and other sharp objects scattered over and alongside the roads. Great numbers of flat tires are very common when this occurs, which means there are even more blockages on the roads.

"Hurricane Wilma's (October 2005) 100-plus mph winds in Miami is forcing these low-quality roofing shingles to stand upright." They were eventually ripped off by the wind. *Photo by author.*

Many traffic lights will be out until electric power has been restored. When possible there will be uniformed officers at major intersections, but any intersection that does not have a working traffic light or someone directing traffic should always be treated as a four-way stop.

If you must be on the road after sundown, drive with extreme caution. No traffic lights also means no street lights. There can be road hazards and people on foot or bicycles you may not easily see, so don't be in a hurry. You should always have a bright flashlight with at least one extra set of batteries in the car at all times anyway, and you are more likely than ever to need it now.

Checking for Damage to Your Home

If at all possible, wait until daylight before starting to assess the damage. Take your time. If you have already determined the extent (or hopefully lack thereof) of damage inside the house, you need to be thorough about examining the exterior as well. This includes the roof, if it is safe to go up there and if you have a sturdy ladder available.

First and foremost, if you have a leaky roof, get it covered with a tarp as quickly as possible. The last thing you need now is more indoor water damage from the rains that are sure to follow over the many days, weeks, or months that will surely pass before you can get a roofing company to start repairs.

Take lots of photos of all damage, from as many angles as possible. An inexpensive digital camera is perfect for this because it is rare nowadays to find an insurance claims adjuster without a laptop computer. It just takes a few minutes to upload your photos, and the adjuster now has solid evidence to back your claim.

Be sure to have the necessary receipts and other documentation to back any claims. Photos of the outside of your house taken before the hurricane can be a great help, too. And by all means get the claim process

Hurricane Charley (2004) damage in Florida; this handmade sign identifies the house for the insurance adjuster. *FEMA photo by Andrea Booher.*

in motion as soon as possible. If your house number is no longer visible, use a hand-painted sign to identify it for the insurance adjuster.

It often happens that in spite of being careful about determining the extent of any damage, something just gets overlooked. Make sure you have an option of later updating your claim if such hidden damage is found.

Trees and Shrubbery

Tree damage or loss is inevitable following any hurricane; it just gets worse during stronger storms. Ornamental plants are frequently damaged as well. If no tree landed on your house, car, boat, or other structure, just consider yourself very lucky and get on with the cleanup.

Even if a tree is blown over, don't assume it is necessarily lost. If the root structure is not completely torn apart, there's a good chance it can be saved. If it's small enough, you may be able to prop it up with a few boards and it's good to go. Big trees require heavy equipment and the services of a professional landscaper, which aren't cheap. But then again, removing, cutting up, and hauling off a downed tree isn't inexpensive either, and after that you will still face the cost of replacing that tree.

Once a downed tree has been righted, watch it carefully over the weeks that follow to make sure it gets sufficient water. Defoliated plants may look dead immediately following the storm, but often all they need is enough water to start growing leaves again.

Most tree loss, as mentioned earlier, can be prevented by keeping them properly trimmed. I do mine every other year in the spring. It makes a big difference. A neighbor failed to keep his properly trimmed, and during Hurricane Andrew in 1992 one of his big trees was split in half and a huge part blown all the way across the stree into my yard. It landed just a few feet from the front of my house. Just a little further, and I almost certainly would have had to deal with some very expensive damage.

Even if you don't lose an entire tree, it's very likely that your yard will become a big trash pile of tree limbs and debris. Getting rid of this mess is a lot of work, and large tree limbs usually require some serious cutting. A chainsaw does this best, if you have one available and if you know how to operate it properly (and safely). But most folks don't realize that a good crosscut saw with big teeth will do the same job with a lot less effort than you might think. It's a lot cheaper to buy, too. And it won't run out of gas or get frozen with rust as long as it is wiped down with oil before being stored, even if it is unused for many months.

As a rule, you'll pile up all debris alongside the road in front of your house for municipal pickup. If there are many big trash piles, as is typical after a bad storm, it may take several months before the cleanup is complete. Just be patient, and keep the street in front of your house as clear as possible.

A good place for roadside trash piles is actually between your house and your neighbor's. If everyone cooperates this way, the front of each house on the entire street remains clearly visible from the road, making it much easier for an insurance adjuster or repair crew to find your address. If your house number was removed or destroyed by the storm, make a new one any way you can.

CHAPTER 16
In the Aftermath

One of the biggest problems following a severe hurricane is widespread looting. Some of these creeps literally come out of the woodwork as soon as the winds begin to subside, while others—sometimes whole families— travel many miles to reach your area. This is yet another good reason for staying home after the storm: as a rule the last thing these thieves want is any confrontation with an upset homeowner.

I've seen several websites that recommend the use of firearms to protect your property. Some actually suggest that you shoot to kill as soon as you even see a suspected looter. Keep your cool; that's a good way to end up in jail. And if you do choose to have a firearm handy, give a lot of thought about how you would use it. The very last thing you want to do is shoot a neighbor or someone who is actually trying to help.

Simply showing that you have a firearm is usually sufficient to discourage any would-be looter. But do not even think about pointing it at anyone unless you

Miami homeowner guarding property from looters following Hurricane Andrew (Category 5, 1992). *FEMA photo by Bob Epstein.*

are in genuine fear of your own safety or that of a family member; otherwise you still risk running afoul of the law. Why survive a hurricane only to end up in jail afterward?

Portable generators are a prime target for looters. If yours isn't in a suitably fenced-in yard, make sure it is secured in place with a bolt cutter–proof lock and chain. Never leave it in plain sight in front of the house. A friend had his snatched that way (it was not chained); it was running at the time, and he heard it suddenly quit. When he reached his front door, he was just in time to see it disappear down the street in the back of a pickup truck.

The Unwanted Invasion

Looters aren't the only thieves who swarm to disaster areas like ants to a picnic. Fake "contractors" come from great distances for the chance to prey on the desperate and unwary. They will promise anything to get a sizeable advance from you, and then disappear without ever starting any work.

Remember, building materials will almost always be in short supply for weeks, if not months, following a major hurricane that generates widespread damage. So beware of the promise to start work within a few days. Also beware of any request for a sizeable advance (50 percent is the typical amount) on a completed price is that is also likely to be greatly inflated. Ask to see a contractor's license, which should come from your state since many states do not allow work by contractors not licensed by them. The same may be true for some counties. Ask for references with telephone numbers.

Take the time to check out anyone you do not know or recognize as being licensed in your area, and be sure to check references. Do not pay with cash in advance, nor with a check made out to "Cash." Reputable contractors will usually request only a small advance, if any at all, and are willing to start billing you when the work is actually started—and sometimes for smaller jobs, not until after it is completed. If you fail to pay a legitimate contractor with a valid license, you'll get a lien on your house, and he knows that.

Even if an unlicensed "contractor" actually does get the job done (or perhaps it looks like it has been completed), the odds are it will be shoddy work, not even close to the requirements of your local building code. Which means you wind up paying for it twice and in the end far more than if you had it done by a licensed contractor in the first place. First there will be the cost of undoing the sloppy work, then the cost of doing it correctly. There is also the possibility of a hefty fine if a county building inspector discovers the substandard work.

Phony contractors caused a huge amount of grief in Miami following Hurricane Andrew in 1992. Many new roofs hastily installed after the storm failed inspection and had to be ripped off and replaced, and other repairs redone. Hundreds of victims lost hundreds of thousands of dollars that were paid in advance for work never even started. Since then, Miami-Dade County has adopted a much tougher attitude toward unlicensed contractors and even out-of-state licensed contractors who fail to meet county requirements. Hopefully other counties have also followed this example. Nevertheless, in the long run your own vigilance is your best defense against getting ripped off.

The Cleanup

Be patient. If the hurricane was severe and covered a large area, it is going to take weeks, maybe even months, for overburdened municipal services to remove all those piles of debris. Remember, the people performing those services have their own problems in the storm's aftermath.

As mentioned earlier, one good way to keep the number of trash piles down is to work with your neighbors and share a common dumping spot between your houses. If everyone did that, the number of piles would be immediately cut in half, saving significant pickup time. Keep those piles as far back from the edge of the street as possible.

You may have trees or sizeable limbs down on your street. Cutting them up into manageable pieces and piling them up off the roadway also clears the way for help. And while a chainsaw might be the desired tool for this, a simple large-tooth hand saw designed for cutting trees is not all that hard to use.

If street signs are down in your neighborhood, try to get them upright as best you can (with your neighbors helping, of course), and the sooner the better. This will greatly aid insurance adjusters, contractors, and other potential assistance workers in finding your house.

When you have time, be sure to police your yard, as well as the sidewalk and street in front, for roofing shingles, and toss them on the trash pile. More often than not these shingles still have roofing nails embedded in them that are quite capable of puncturing tires and even hard-soled shoes. Getting a tetanus shot or a tire repair is not easy at a time like this, and often more than one tire gets flattened at the same time. Then what will you do for a spare?

Watch out for downed power lines while you work outside. You never know when they might be "live," even if the area is apparently without electricity. Far too many have died this way in years past after surviving the full wrath of a major hurricane.

Don't Drive Unnecessarily

I cannot say this too often or too strongly: Stay off the roads unless you absolutely have to drive. Gasoline will be in short supply for at least several days, and maybe longer since only those stations with emergency generators will be able to run their pumps until power is restored in your area, no matter how much gasoline they might have in their underground tanks. Getting more fuel delivered to these stations may also take a while if local supplies are low.

Many traffic lights will be out until power is restored, creating real hazards at major intersections. Police or members of the National Guard may man these intersections to direct traffic, but you can bet there will not be enough of them to take care of every one that does not have an operational traffic light. Plus, several days of rainy weather often follow a hurricane event, making road conditions even more difficult, and ponding water on roadways is yet another hazard to be dealt with.

Then there are also those thoughtless, impatient drivers who seem to feel they should always have the right-of-way. The numbers of accidents they cause skyrockets, and already overloaded law enforcement agencies just cannot keep up with this extra load. You could be stuck for many hours in an accident that was not your fault and that blocks the road so that no one gets through.

So think before you act in all situations. The incredible amount of destruction that follows a major hurricane hides numerous hazards.

CHAPTER 17
Disaster Relief Services

The Federal Emergency Management Agency (FEMA) has certainly had its public relations ups and downs in the arena of hurricane disasters, but essentially it is there to help. Yes, it was caught unprepared for the magnitude of the New Orleans disaster following Hurricane Katrina in 2005, but then no one else expected anything close to that enormous amount of damage, either. And yes, FEMA is still a work in progress, but a great many of us have not helped—in fact, some have even severely hindered—the process of disaster relief development through our own actions or inactions. To a large extent we have only ourselves to blame, since far too many of us have been very lax about our own pre-storm preparations, assuming that we don't really have to do it ourselves since the Feds will be there to bail us out. By now some valuable lessons about this should have been learned.

Contrary to popular belief, FEMA has neither unlimited resources nor unlimited manpower. Like every other

Lining up for assistance after Hurricane Andrew (Category 5, 1992).
FEMA photo by Bob Epstein.

government organization in this country, it has a budget. In theory it should really be considered an agency of last resort, someone to turn to after we have exhausted our own survival resources. By asking FEMA for help when we should not really require it, we are only self-ishly diminishing that agency's capacity to help those in genuine need.

One example is the failure to have adequate amounts of drinking water and ice on hand before the storm arrives. This seems like a small problem if considered individually, but when multiplied by the thou-sands who line up for those items immediately after a hurricane has passed, the cost is staggering. At the other extreme are those scofflaws so greedy they don't hesitate to file false claims for financial assistance for damage than never occurred. As I write this book the Feds are still vigorously prosecuting false claims made following hurricanes Charley (2004), Katrina (2005), Wilma (2005), and others.

If you feel you have a genuine need for FEMA assistance, you can contact that agency by telephone at (800)621-FEMA(3362). For those with speech or hearing difficulties, the TTY number is (800)462-7585. Expect these lines to be very busy following a major hurricane, so be patient and keep trying, or try the American Red Cross (see page 198 and 199).

If you have the means, make your initial application or check its status online at *www.fema.gov*. Registering online is one of the best methods to complete an application and avoid busy signals on the telephone. If you gather the required information prior to starting the application, the process should take approximately 20 minutes.

If you do not have access to an Internet-connected computer, check your local library or disaster recovery center where computers or kiosks may be available. Or, call a friend or relative outside the area affected by the storm and have them apply for assistance via the Internet on your behalf. FEMA can accept an application from any person but will only provide follow-up information to the individual needing assistance. Applicants should share personal information only with trusted individuals.

Keep in mind that an Internet application process expires after 30 minutes as a security precaution, and information entered will be lost if you do not complete the process within this time period. Thus you are strongly advised to have all of the information you need at hand before starting the process.

All you need to do to check the status of your application online is to log in to the Online Individual Assistance Center. Use the pin and password that were created when you registered. If you registered by phone, you can easily create an account to check the status of your application online.

The American Red Cross is required by congressional charter to undertake relief activities to ease the suffering caused by a disaster. Emergency assistance includes fixed or mobile feeding stations, shelter, cleaning supplies, comfort kits, first aid, blood and blood products, food, clothing, emergency transportation, rent payment assistance, home repairs, household items, and medical supplies. Additional assistance for long-term recovery may be provided when other relief assistance and/or personal resources are not adequate to meet disaster-caused needs. The American Red Cross provides referrals to government and other agencies providing disaster assistance. If you cannot reach the local Red Cross office by telephone, the national toll-free number is (877)725-0400. And by the way, if you do not need help yourself but would like to help others who are not so fortunate, consider donating money or goods to this very worthy organization.

The Salvation Army provides emergency assistance including mass and mobile feeding, temporary shelter, counseling, missing person services, medical assistance, and distribution of donated goods including food, clothing, and household items. It also provides referrals to government and private agencies for special services. Consider this proven organization as well if you are able to make a donation.

Others Who Are There to Help

According to FEMA, the following agencies also often play a major role in disaster assistance. Not all of these are available in any given area. Since many are affiliated with or sponsored by various religious organizations, you should start there when contacting them. For others, you will probably have to do some searching to find them.

- *The Adventist Community Services (ACS)* receives, processes, and distributes clothing, bedding, and food products. In major disasters, the agency brings in mobile distribution units filled with bedding and packaged clothing that is pre-sorted according to size, age, and gender. ACS also provides emergency food and counseling and participates in the cooperative disaster child-care program.

- ***The American Radio Relay League, Inc. (ARRL)*** is a national volunteer organization of licensed radio amateurs in the United States. ARRL-sponsored Amateur Radio Emergency Services (ARES) provide volunteer radio communications services to Federal, state, county, and local governments, as well as to voluntary agencies. Members volunteer not only their services but also their privately owned radio communications equipment.

- ***The Ananda Marga Universal Relief Team (AMURT)*** renders immediate medical care, food and clothing distribution, stress management, and community and social services. AMURT also provides long-term development assistance and sustainable economic programs to help disaster-affected people. AMURT depends primarily on full- and part-time volunteer help, and has a large volunteer base to draw on worldwide. AMURT provides and encourages disaster services training in conjunction with other relief agencies like the American Red Cross.

- ***The Catholic Charities USA Disaster Response*** is the organization that unites the social services agencies operated by most of the 175 Catholic dioceses in the United States. The Disaster Response section of Catholic Charities USA provides assistance to communities in addressing the crisis and recovery needs of local families. Catholic Charities agencies emphasize ongoing and long-term recovery services for individuals and families, including temporary housing assistance for low income families, counseling programs for children and the elderly, and special counseling for disaster relief workers.

- *The Christian Disaster Response (CDR)* worked in cooperation with the American Red Cross, the Salvation Army, Church World Service Disaster Response, and NOVAD to enable local church members to become effective volunteers for assignment on national disasters. CDR provides disaster assessments, fixed or mobile feeding facilities, and in-kind disaster relief supplies. CDR also coordinates and stockpiles the collection of donated goods through their regional centers throughout the United States.
- *The Christian Reformed World Relief Committee (CRWRC)* has the overall aim of assisting churches in the disaster-affected community to respond to the needs of persons within that community. CRWRC provides advocacy services to assist disaster victims in finding permanent, long-

term solutions to their disaster-related problems, as well as housing repair and construction, needs assessment, cleanup, child care, and other recovery services.

- **_The Church of the Brethren Disaster Response_** provides cleanup and debris removal from damaged or destroyed homes and personal property. Volunteers are trained through the Cooperative Disaster Child Care Program to establish child-care centers following major disasters. Child-care providers guide children through activities that help them to act out their fears, anger, and confusion following a disaster. Many denominations support this program.

- **_The Church World Service (CWS) Disaster Response_** assists disaster survivors through inter-religious partner organizations in the United States and worldwide on behalf of its 32 member communions plus affiliated agencies. CWS Disaster Response comprises consultants who help convene local churches and religious organization to coordinate responses to unmet needs during the recovery phase.

- **_The Episcopal Church Presiding Bishop's Fund for World Relief_** responds to domestic disasters principally through its network of nearly 100 U.S. dioceses and over 8,200 parishes. It also sends immediate relief grants for such basics as food, water, medical assistance, and financial aid within the first 90 days following a disaster. Ongoing recovery activities are provided through rehabilitation grants, which offer the means to rebuild, replant ruined crops, and counsel those in trauma. The Episcopal Church works primarily through Church World Service in providing its disaster-related services.

- ***The International Relief Friendship Foundation (IRFF)*** has the fundamental goal of assisting agencies involved in responding to the needs of a community after disaster strikes. When a disaster hits, IRFF mobilizes a volunteer group from universities, businesses, youth groups, women's organizations, and religious groups. IRFF also provides direct support and emergency services immediately following a disaster such as blankets, food, clothing, and relief kits.

- ***The Lutheran Disaster Response (LDR)*** provides for immediate disaster response in both natural and technological disasters, long-term rebuilding efforts, and support for preparedness planning through synods, districts, and social ministry organizations. The disasters to which LDR responds are those in which needs outstrip available local resources. LDR provides for the coordination of 6,000 volunteers annually. In addition, LDR provides crisis counseling, support groups, mental health assistance, and pastoral care through its accredited social service agencies.

- *Mennonite Disaster Services* assists disaster victims by providing volunteer personnel to clean up and remove debris from damaged and destroyed homes and personal property and to repair or rebuild homes. Special emphasis is placed on assisting those less able to help themselves, such as the elderly and handicapped.
- *The National Emergency Response Team (NERT)* meets the basic human needs of shelter, food, and clothing during times of crisis and disaster. NERT provides Emergency Mobile Trailer units (EMTUs), which are self-contained, modest living units for up to 8 to 10 people, to places where disaster occurs. When EMTUs are not in use as homes, they serve as mobile teaching units used in Emergency Preparedness programs in communities.
- *The National Organization for Victim Assistance* provides social and mental health services for individuals and families who experience major trauma after disaster, including critical incident debriefings.
- *The Nazarene Disaster Response* provides cleanup and rebuilding assistance, especially to the elderly, disabled, widowed, and those least able to help themselves. In addition, a National Crisis

Counseling Coordinator works into the recovery phase by assisting with the emotional needs of disaster victims.

- ***The Presbyterian Disaster Assistance*** works primarily through Church World Service in providing volunteers to serve as disaster consultants and funding for local recovery projects that meet certain guidelines. This agency also provides trained volunteers who participate in the Cooperative Disaster Child Care program. On a local level, many Presbyterians provide volunteer labor and material assistance.

- ***The REACT International*** provides emergency communication facilities for other agencies through its national network of Citizens' Band radio operators and volunteer teams. REACT encourages its teams to become part of their local disaster preparedness plan. Furthermore, it encourages them to take first-aid training and to become proficient in communications in time of disaster.

- ***The Second Harvest National Network of Food Banks*** collects, transports, warehouses, and distributes donated food and grocery products for other agencies involved in both feeding operations and the distribution of relief supplies through its national network of food banks. Second Harvest also processes food products collected in food drives by communities wishing to help another disaster-affected community. Second Harvest develops, certifies, and supports its food banks; serves as a liaison between the food banks and the donors; and educates the public about the problems and solutions of hunger.

- **The Society of St. Vincent de Paul** provides social services to individuals and families, and collects and distributes donated goods. It operates retail stores, homeless shelters, and feeding facilities that are similar to those run by the Salvation Army. The stores' merchandise can be made available to disaster victims. Warehousing facilities are used for storing and sorting donated merchandise during the emergency period.

- **The Southern Baptist Disaster Relief** provides more than 200 mobile feeding units staffed by volunteers who can prepare and distribute thousands of meals a day. Active in providing disaster child care, the agency has several mobile child-care units. Southern Baptists also assist with cleanup activities, temporary repairs, reconstruction, counseling, and bilingual services.

- **The United Methodist Committee on Relief** provides funding for local units in response and recovery projects based on the needs of each situation. This agency also provides spiritual and emotional care to disaster victims and long-term care of children impacted by disaster.

- ***The United States Service Command*** provides trained corps to voluntary and governmental agencies during disaster.
- ***The Volunteers of America*** is involved in initial response services aimed at meeting the critical needs of disaster victims, such as making trucks available for transporting victims and supplies to designated shelters. It also collects and distributes donated goods and provides mental health care for survivors of disaster.

POSTSCRIPT
The Eye of the Storm

Following Hurricane Betsy in 1965, Miami, Florida enjoyed 22 "hurricane free" years, suffering nothing worse than a weak tropical storm or two, and a few near misses with hurricanes that passed well to the east as they re-curved northward. This is far below the statistical probability for the area, and many of us feared that eventually law of averages would be reasserted.

During this lull, local home builders successfully lobbied for less stringent building codes, insisting that "hurricanes do not come here any more." Up until then Miami-Dade County had the strongest windstorm building codes in the world, but they were being systematically weakened, nibbled away bit by bit. By 1992 weak codes, along with lax code enforcement, and in some cases shoddy construction, set the stage for a disaster of epic proportions.

Sure enough, disaster responded to this open invitation in the form of Hurricane Andrew. The 1992 hurricane season had been unusually slow up to this point, and then Andrew formed in the eastern Atlantic on August 16 as a tropical depression in an area that has historically spawned a great number of very strong hurricanes. By August 20, Andrew had grown into a Category 1 hurricane with 75 mph winds. Strengthening continued, and on August 23 it was declared a Category 5 with 175 mph winds. Now a monster storm, it traveled northwestward to just east of the Bahamas before turning due west toward south Florida. The eye eventually came ashore in south Florida with 165 mph winds and a storm surge of 16 to 18 feet.

I had just returned from two weeks in Alaska to learn that Andrew was expected to hit Miami in three days. Fortunately long before then, because of a hurricane threat some years earlier, I already had pre-cut pieces of heavy plywood to fit all the windows in my house and stored them in the garage. By late afternoon of August 23, just hours before Andrew's expected arrival, every window was covered and all other preparations were completed.

We did not have long to wait. Shortly after dark the winds began to increase and rain squalls began coming ashore. By midnight Andrew was upon us; the power was out (which would last for a week) and the winds had already increased to over 100 mph in gusts. Each new gust seemed to reach a higher velocity with a corresponding increase in noise. By 4 a.m. the wind was roaring like a 747 with all engines revved to the max, as if it were trying to push its way through the front of the house! Everything was shaking; tree limbs were flying around like missiles, banging into the plywood window covers like sledge hammers.

Stronger and stronger squalls began to come more frequently, each one increasing in both intensity and duration. High-velocity winds drove the rain horizontally with the power of a fire hose, forcing water through every opening it could find. About this time I briefly peeked into the garage and saw the big steel door bulging substantially inward with each gust. At this point I could not see how it could get any worse—but it did. The noise and pounding kept escalating to levels that made it almost impossible to think. Even though my house was built in 1968 to the older, more stringent Miami-Dade County code, I nevertheless became very fearful that it could not stand up to this intense abuse.

Andrew's fury peaked at my house around 5 a.m. with gusts that likely exceeded 150 mph. Just a few miles south of me the strongest surface gust was unofficially measured at 212 mph, just before the building and anemometer were destroyed.

Daylight finally began to penetrate the thick clouds around 630 a.m., and by then it was obvious the worst was over. Two hours later the winds had decreased to less than 30 mph. It had been the longest, most terrifying night of my entire life!

I was very, very lucky. If my windows had not been properly protected, one or more would surely have imploded and the full strength of the storm would have been inside my house with immediate catastrophic results. Or, if that heavily braced big steel garage door had failed, the outcome would have likely been the same. The roof might not have held in spite of all the heavy tiedown straps. Also fortunately, I had replaced the roof shingles only a year earlier—so they held. If they had come off I would have had a house full of water.

At one point during the peak of the storm, a very large black olive tree on the other side of the street split in two at the point where the trunk forked, and that half of the tree landed just a few feet from my front door—truly a disaster narrowly averted.

Although Andrew was small in size, it was still an extremely intense hurricane with its most destructive winds largely confined to a band that measured just a little over 20 miles wide in its northern semicircle. The eye came ashore near Homestead, 25 miles south of Miami, and passed right over the Turkey Point Nuclear Power Plant—less than 18 miles south of my house. The building that houses the reactors, designed to withstand winds in excess of 225 mph, was fortunately never breached.

Hurricane Andrew is so far only the third Category 5 storm to make landfall in the U.S. since accurate records have been kept. It was also the first multi-billion dollar hurricane, doing almost 41 billion dollars' worth of damage and claiming 39 lives in Florida and Louisiana. To this day, only Hurricane Katrina in 2005 was more costly ($89.6 billion, 1,833 lives) when it hit the northern coast of the Gulf of Mexico. Most of this was due to extensive flooding in New Orleans. Katrina was "only" a Category 3 with 125 mph winds at the time, but as always in these situations most of the real damage and loss of life was caused by water.